I0418495

# SOCIAL SKILLS FOR TEENS

A Parent's Guide to Helping Teens Overcome
Challenges with Online Communication, Social Anxiety,
Self Esteem, and Peer Pressure

---

## AMBER PRESTON

© **Copyright 2024 - All rights reserved.**

The content contained within this book may not be reproduced, duplicated or transmitted without direct written permission from the author or the publisher.

Under no circumstances will any blame or legal responsibility be held against the publisher, or author, for any damages, reparation, or monetary loss due to the information contained within this book, either directly or indirectly.

**Legal Notice:**

This book is copyright protected. It is only for personal use. You cannot amend, distribute, sell, use, quote or paraphrase any part, or the content within this book, without the consent of the author or publisher.

**Disclaimer Notice:**

Please note the information contained within this document is for educational and entertainment purposes only. All effort has been executed to present accurate, up to date, reliable, complete information. No warranties of any kind are declared or implied. Readers acknowledge that the author is not engaged in the rendering of legal, financial, medical or professional advice. The content within this book has been derived from various sources. Please consult a licensed professional before attempting any techniques outlined in this book.

By reading this document, the reader agrees that under no circumstances is the author responsible for any losses, direct or indirect, that are incurred as a result of the use of the information contained within this document, including, but not limited to, errors, omissions, or inaccuracies.

# Table of Contents

# Introduction

In today's digital age, where emojis often replace genuine emotions and online comments substitute for face-to-face conversations, the art of authentic connection seems to be fading into the background, especially for our teenagers. As someone who has dedicated years to understanding and enhancing adolescents' social skills, I've witnessed firsthand the unique challenges that come with growing up in this digital whirlwind.

My journey into this field wasn't a coincidence, but a path paved as I've watched teenagers show up and wrestle with the messy reality of human connection in both digital and face-to-face spaces. Through their struggles and successes, I realized there was an urgent need for a guide that addresses the nuances of modern communication and the social challenges teens face today.

This book is born from that realization—a toolkit designed to bridge the gap between digital natives and their parents. What sets this resource apart is its focus on practical, actionable advice for identifying the root causes of social anxiety, cultivating empathy, and fostering genuine connections. The innovative "Adult-Teen

Exercises" at the end of each chapter provide a unique opportunity for parents and teens to grow together.

So, why did you pick up this book? Ask yourself:

- Do you worry about your teen's ability to form meaningful relationships in a world dominated by screens?
- Are you concerned that your child might be missing out on crucial social skills due to excessive online interaction?
- Do you want to help your teen navigate the complexities of modern social dynamics but feel ill-equipped to do so?

If you answered yes to any of these questions, then this guide has found its way to you for a reason. As a parent, you have unique concerns that keep you up at night. Whether it's quiet dinners, closed bedroom doors, or fears about your child losing real human contact, this book is designed specifically with you and your concerns in mind.

Throughout these pages, we'll explore key social skills vital to any teenager's development. Each skill is supported by engaging activities that guarantee not just learning, but also connection. The compelling statistics and heartwarming anecdotes sprinkled throughout aren't just numbers or stories—they're windows into the realities faced by families worldwide, including yours.

This isn't just a book to read; it's a manual to interact with. The "Adult-Teen Exercise" sections provide opportunities for you and your teen to connect, learn, and grow together. By applying the tools and tips discussed here, you can expect to see real improvements in your teenager's confidence, interactive abilities, and overall happiness.

I'm inviting you to join me in this work. This is your chance to profoundly shape how your child connects and thrives. Together, we can nurture honest, grounded relationships in our screen-filled world.

Are you ready to help your teen tap into their authentic social self? Turn the page, and let's begin. It won't always be smooth sailing, but that's where growth happens.

ONE

# The Digital Age and Its Impact

D id you know that the average teen spends up to nine hours daily on screens, with a significant chunk devoted to social media and messaging apps? This isn't just a statistic; it's a window into how profoundly the digital world has reshaped the way our teens communicate and connect. The shift from lively dinner table conversations to silent, screen-focused gatherings isn't just a change in dynamics; it's a complete overhaul of communication practices that previous generations could hardly imagine. Understanding these changes and adapting our approach as parents is crucial in fostering healthy communication habits and maintaining strong connections with our kids.

In this chapter, we'll learn about the various facets of this digital revolution and its impact on our teens' lives. From the emergence of new communication platforms to the challenges of maintaining a healthy online-offline balance, we'll navigate the complexities of raising teens in the digital age. Let's get started and uncover the tools and strategies we need to guide our children through this ever-evolving landscape.

### The Shift to Online Communication: Navigating the New Norm

The digital revolution has fundamentally altered the way our teens interact with the world around them. As parents, it's crucial that we understand this shift to effectively guide our children through the complexities of modern communication. Let's examine the key aspects of this new norm and how we can adapt our parenting strategies accordingly.

With the rise of digital platforms, teen communication has undergone a seismic shift. Instagram, Snapchat, TikTok, and WhatsApp aren't just apps—they're the primary tools for adolescent interactions. This shift isn't merely about technology replacing traditional forms of communication; it represents a fundamental change in how teens develop socially. These platforms aren't just stages for socializing; they're arenas where social skills are shaped and tested.

As we move forward, it's important to recognize that these digital platforms are more than just passing trends. They're the new social playground for our teens, and understanding their role is crucial for effective parenting in the digital age.

The transition from direct conversations to digital exchanges has significant implications for developing social skills. In digital communications, the immediate feedback loop that face-to-face interaction provides—through gestures, facial expressions, and tone - is often diluted or entirely absent. This can lead to misunderstandings and a decrease in the ability to read emotional cues, which are essential for developing empathy and maintaining relationships.

Recognizing these changes in communication patterns allows us to better understand the challenges our teens face in developing and maintaining relationships in the digital world. It also highlights the importance of ensuring they have opportunities for face-to-face interactions to develop well-rounded communication skills.

Navigating this new norm goes beyond monitoring screen time or supervising social media accounts; it requires a fundamental understanding of the digital landscape and its language. Start by engaging with the platforms your teen uses—not to spy, but to understand the context and nuances of their digital interactions. This engagement can help bridge the generational gap, offering insights into your teen's social world.

By adapting to this digital landscape ourselves, we're better equipped to guide our teens through it. This approach allows us to have more informed and meaningful conversations about their online experiences.

To foster healthier online habits, encourage your teens to engage in meaningful digital interactions that enrich their lives. Discuss the importance of quality over quantity in online communications, emphasizing connections that foster positive feedback and authentic interactions. You can also co-create a digital wellness plan that includes scheduled offline times, ensuring that digital habits align with overall well-being.

As we move forward, remember that promoting healthy online habits is an ongoing process. It requires open communication, flexibility, and a willingness to learn and adapt alongside our teens.

## Understanding Social Media's Role in Your Teen's Life

Social media has become an integral part of our teens' lives, shaping their social interactions, self-expression, and identity formation. To effectively guide our children through this digital landscape, we need to understand the multifaceted role that social media plays in their world. Let's examine the various aspects of social media's influence and how we can help our teens navigate this complex terrain.

For today's teens, social media isn't just a platform; it's a vibrant ecosystem where they thrive, socialize, and express themselves. It serves as a social life line that goes beyond mere entertainment—it's where identities are forged and reshaped. In these digital spaces, teenagers find a venue for connection that transcends the physical boundaries of their local environment.

Understanding social media's role as a social lifeline helps us appreciate its significance in our teens' lives. This perspective allows us to approach discussions about social media use with empathy and insight.

However, the pervasive influence of social media comes with its own set of challenges. The platform that allows teens to connect and explore can also expose them to the pressures of comparison culture, where the curated highlights of others' lives can lead to unrealistic standards for personal achievement and happiness. This phenomenon can skew one's self-perception and exacerbate underlying insecurities.

Recognizing both the benefits and potential pitfalls of social media use is crucial. It allows us to have balanced conversations with our teens about their online experiences and helps us guide them towards healthy digital habits.

Navigating these interactions and influences requires a nuanced approach that goes beyond simply monitoring social media usage. The goal is to mentor rather than monitor, guiding teens through the intricacies of online interactions without making them feel surveilled.

It's about fostering an environment where teens feel comfortable sharing their online experiences, allowing you to provide guidance and support when they encounter challenging situations.

By shifting our approach from monitoring to mentoring, we can build trust and open communication with our teens about their online lives. This approach allows us to be more effective in guiding them through the digital landscape.

Encourage teens to gravitate towards positive online communities —spaces that affirm their worth, respect their ideas, and foster constructive interactions. Help them explore various platforms to identify communities that align with their interests and values, whether it's art, music, science, or social activism.

Remember that understanding social media's role in your teen's life is an ongoing process. Stay curious, keep the lines of communication open, and be ready to adapt your approach as the digital landscape continues to evolve.

## Digital Etiquette: Teaching Respect and Kindness Online

In the digital world, where face-to-face interactions are often replaced by screen-to-screen communications, teaching our teens about digital etiquette is more important than ever. This section will explore how we can instill values of respect, kindness, and responsible behavior in our teens' online interactions. Let's learn more about the key aspects of digital etiquette and how we can effectively teach these crucial skills.

Digital citizenship is a crucial framework for guiding behavior in this connected world. It encompasses aspects like digital literacy, ethics, etiquette, and online safety. Understanding and embracing good digital citizenship is essential because it sets the tone for how individuals, especially vulnerable teens, interact in their digital worlds.

By emphasizing the importance of digital citizenship, we lay the foundation for responsible and respectful online behavior. This understanding helps our teens navigate the digital world with confidence and integrity.

In an era where empathy can sometimes be diluted by the digital divide—where screens shield us from the immediate emotional reactions of those we interact with—it's crucial to actively cultivate a sense of empathy and respect in online interactions. Remind your teen that there's always a real person behind the screen, with feelings, hopes, and vulnerabilities just like their own. Start by discussing real scenarios teens might encounter online, such as witnessing or experiencing cyberbullying. Ask your child how they would feel if they were to imagine being in the other person's shoes, and discuss the power of words in both positive and negative contexts.

By focusing on empathy, we help our teens develop the emotional intelligence needed to navigate online interactions with kindness and understanding. This skill is invaluable not just in the digital world, but in all aspects of life.

Parents have a unique opportunity to model positive digital conduct. This goes beyond not texting while driving or avoiding oversharing personal information on social media; it's also about demonstrating mindfulness and respect in every digital communication. Show your teen that even a simple 'please' or 'thank you' can change the tone of a digital exchange, and that addressing misunderstandings calmly and clearly can prevent many online conflicts.

Remember, our teens are watching and learning from our online behavior. By setting a positive example, we reinforce the importance of digital etiquette in a powerful and tangible way.

It's inevitable that teens will eventually encounter negative comments or cyberbullying. Teaching them how to handle these experiences constructively is crucial to ensuring they don't become overwhelmed or hurt by such incidents. Encourage your teen to come to you or another trusted adult if they experience anything upsetting online. Discuss strategies for managing negativity, such as not responding to provocative comments, blocking users who are consistently negative, and reporting serious cases of cyberbullying to both platform administrators and, if necessary, local authorities.

Teaching these skills is an ongoing process. Regularly revisit these topics with your teen, and be open to learning from their experiences as well. By fostering a culture of respect and kindness online, we help create a more positive digital world for everyone.

### The Balance Between Online and Offline: Finding Harmony

In our increasingly connected world, striking a balance between online engagement and offline activities is crucial for our teens' well-being. It's important to learn about and develop strategies for helping our children find harmony between their digital and real-world experiences. Doing this can encourage a healthy balance that allows our teens to benefit from both worlds.

In the rhythm of our daily lives, where screens often dominate our attention and interactions, the importance of finding balance between digital engagement and the real world couldn't be more significant. While the digital world is rich with information and communities, it can't capture the nuances of human interaction that are only nurtured through face-to-face engagement.

Understanding the need for balance is the first step in helping our teens navigate their online and offline worlds. It sets the stage for creating strategies that promote a well-rounded lifestyle.

Designate specific areas or times of the day as tech-free—for example, during meal times or in the family living room in the evening. This encourages everyone to engage with each other without the distractions of phones, tablets, or laptops. The goal is to create environments that foster connection through conversation, board games, cooking together, or other group activities that encourage cooperation and communication.

By creating these unplugged spaces, we provide opportunities for genuine face-to-face interactions and help our teens develop crucial social skills that can't be replicated online.

Motivating teens to explore real-world hobbies and interests plays a significant role in balancing online and offline activities. Whether it's sports, music, art, or reading, hobbies can significantly enrich a teen's life, providing fulfillment and skills that might not be developed online. Support their endeavors by attending their performances, games, or simply providing the resources they need to pursue these activities.

Engaging in offline hobbies not only provides a break from screen time but also helps teens develop new skills, build confidence, and discover passions that can enrich their lives in meaningful ways.

Encourage your teens to participate in group activities where they can interact with peers in various settings. These could be study groups, community service initiatives, or social gatherings like family get-togethers or neighborhood picnics. Each setting offers different dynamics and opportunities for developing social skills.

Helping your teen find balance requires flexibility, open communication, and a willingness to adjust strategies as they grow and their needs change. By promoting a healthy balance between online and offline activities, we help our teens develop into well-rounded individuals capable of thriving in both digital and real-world environments.

## Screen Time vs. Face Time: Encouraging Real Connections

In the age of digital communication, the value of face-to-face interactions can sometimes be overlooked. Helping teens understand the importance of real connections and providing them strategies for encouraging meaningful in-person interactions alongside digital communication is crucial to help our teens strike a balance between screen time and facetime.

In-person interactions foster a range of non-verbal cues that digital communication can't replicate. These include body language, tone of voice, and immediate feedback, all of which are crucial for understanding emotional nuances and developing empathy. When teens interact face-to-face, they learn how to navigate the subtleties of human emotions and reactions, which are essential for building strong personal and professional relationships in the future.

Understanding the unique value of face-to-face communication helps us emphasize its importance to our teens. It sets the stage for encouraging more in-person interactions in their daily lives.

Fostering this balance as parents doesn't mean imposing strict rules that might be met with resistance, but rather guiding your teens with agreed-upon boundaries that they understand and see the value in. One effective strategy is the co-creation of a "family media plan," This plan involves setting clear guidelines for when and where screens can be used at home, as well as ensuring that digital devices don't interfere with sleep, study, or family interaction times.

By involving our teens in the process of setting screen time limits, we empower them to take ownership of their digital habits and understand the importance of balance.

Shifting focus from quantity to quality in digital communication can also significantly enhance relationships. Discuss the importance of being present during digital interactions with your teen. This can mean having more meaningful video calls with family or friends rather than frequent, fragmented text exchanges. Demonstrate the value of full attention during these calls, comparing it to what they would offer someone face-to-face.

Encouraging real connections in a digital world is an ongoing effort, requiring patience, understanding, and a willingness to lead by example. By emphasizing the value of face-to-face interactions and helping our teens find a balance with their screen time, we equip them with the skills they need to build strong, meaningful relationships both online and offline.

### Exercise: Digital Wellness Plan

Now that we've explored the various aspects of navigating the digital world, let's put our knowledge into action. This activity is designed to help you and your teen work together to create a personalized approach to digital wellness. It's an opportunity to open up dialogue, set mutual expectations, and create a plan that works for your family.

This activity is not about imposing rules, but rather about collaboratively creating a framework that supports your teen's digital well-being. It's an opportunity to demonstrate that you value their input and trust their judgment, while also providing guidance and support.

*Objective*

Create a personalized digital wellness plan with your teen to promote healthy online habits and a balanced digital lifestyle.

**Instructions**

1. Sit down with your teen for an open and honest discussion about their current online activities.

- Ask them what aspects of their digital life they enjoy and find meaningful.
- Encourage them to share any concerns or areas they feel could be improved.

2. Based on your conversation, work together to establish guidelines for healthy digital practices. Consider including:

- Specific times for unplugging, such as during meals, before bedtime, or for a set period each day.
- Ideas for balancing online and offline activities, like setting aside time for hobbies, outdoor play, or face-to-face socializing.
- Strategies for engaging in digital practices that are enriching and meaningful, such as learning a new skill, connecting with friends and family, or exploring creative outlets.

3. Create a shared digital calendar or document where you can record your agreed-upon digital wellness plan.

- Include the specific guidelines, schedules, and activities you've discussed.
- Make sure both you and your teen have access to this plan for easy reference and accountability.

4. Schedule regular check-ins to review the plan together, perhaps once a week or every few weeks.

- Discuss what's working well and what challenges you've encountered.
- Make adjustments to the plan as needed, based on your teen's needs and evolving digital landscape.
- Celebrate successes and encourage open communication about digital wellness.

**Reflection**

After implementing your digital wellness plan for a month, reflect on the experience together:

- What positive changes have you noticed in your teen's digital habits and overall well-being?
- What strategies have been most effective in promoting a balanced digital lifestyle?
- What areas still need improvement, and how can you continue to support your teen's healthy relationship with technology?

By engaging your teen in open dialogue, setting clear guidelines, and regularly reviewing progress, you can help them develop the skills and mindset needed to navigate the digital world in a healthy, balanced way.

As we conclude this chapter, it's important to remember that navigating the digital world with our teens isn't about being perfect—it's about being present, curious, and open to learning together. The digital landscape is constantly evolving, and so must our approaches to parenting within it. By understanding their digital world, fostering open communication, and working together to create healthy habits, we can help our teens develop the skills they need to thrive both online and offline.

The journey of parenting in the digital age is complex and often challenging, but it's also filled with opportunities for connection, growth, and mutual understanding. As we move forward, let's approach this journey with patience, flexibility, and a commitment to supporting our teens as they navigate the intricate web of digital and real-world interactions. Together, we can help them build the foundation for a balanced, fulfilling life in our increasingly connected world.

# TWO

## Social Anxiety in Teens

Did you know that about 9% of teens experience social anxiety disorder? (Leigh & Clark, 2018). That's not just a statistic—it's a window into the silent struggle many of our kids face every day. As parents, we often chalk up our teens' reluctance to socialize to typical adolescent awkwardness. But sometimes, it's more than that. It's a deep-seated fear that can profoundly impact their lives.

In this chapter, we'll start to understand social anxiety in teens. We'll learn what it looks like, where it comes from, and most importantly, how we can help our kids navigate through it. Whether your teen is dealing with mild social discomfort or more severe anxiety, you'll find practical strategies and insights to support them on their journey to social confidence.

### Identifying Social Anxiety: Signs and Symptoms

Social anxiety isn't just about being shy or introverted. It's an intense, persistent fear of being watched and judged by others.

While shyness might make someone uncomfortable in social situations, social anxiety can be debilitating, making even the simplest daily activities feel impossible.

Think about the last time you felt nervous before a big presentation or meeting new people. Now, imagine feeling that level of anxiety every time you step out of the house or interact with others. That's the reality for many teens with social anxiety.

So, what does social anxiety look like in teens? It might show up as:

- Avoiding school or social activities
- Physical symptoms like shaking, sweating, or nausea in social situations
- Difficulty speaking to strangers or authority figures
- Extreme fear of embarrassment or humiliation
- Reluctance to eat in public or use public restrooms
- Refusing to participate in class discussions
- Excessive worry about upcoming social events
- Overanalyzing their performance after social interactions
- Difficulty making eye contact or speaking above a whisper
- Preferring to communicate via text or social media rather than in person

These aren't just occasional nerves—they're persistent fears that don't subside and often worsen over time without intervention.

It's important to note that these symptoms can vary from teen to teen. Some might experience all of these signs, while others might only show a few. The key is to look for patterns and persistence in these behaviors.

The impact of social anxiety on a teen's life can be far-reaching. Academically, they might struggle not because they lack understanding, but because their fear of being called on or presenting in class is paralyzing. They might avoid asking teachers for help, leading to misunderstandings and poor grades. Group projects can become a source of immense stress, potentially affecting not just their own performance but also their relationships with classmates.

Socially, they might have few friends, not because they're uninterested in relationships, but because their fear of social interactions is overwhelming. They might miss out on parties, school dances, or other social events that are crucial for developing social skills and building connections. This isolation can lead to feelings of loneliness and depression, further exacerbating their anxiety.

At home, family dynamics can be affected too. Family gatherings might become a source of tension, with the teen withdrawing or becoming irritable. Parents and siblings might feel frustrated or helpless, not understanding why their loved one is struggling so much with what seems like everyday interactions.

When should you seek help? If you notice your teen consistently avoiding social situations, experiencing intense fear before social events, or if their anxiety is significantly interfering with their daily life, it might be time to consult a professional. Here are some specific signs that professional help might be needed:

- Your teen's anxiety is causing them to miss school regularly
- They're unable to make or maintain friendships due to their anxiety
- Their fears are interfering with family relationships or activities
- They're showing signs of depression or talking about self-harm

- Their anxiety is leading to physical symptoms like chronic headaches or stomach aches
- They're using alcohol or drugs to cope with social situations

Remember, seeking help isn't a sign of weakness or failure. It's a proactive step towards helping your teen live a fuller, happier life. Many teens with social anxiety benefit greatly from cognitive-behavioral therapy, and in some cases, medication might be recommended. A mental health professional can provide a proper diagnosis and create a tailored treatment plan for your teen.

## The Roots of Social Anxiety: Understanding Causes

Social anxiety doesn't have a single cause. It's usually a complex interplay of biological and environmental factors. Understanding these root causes can help us approach the problem with more empathy and develop more effective strategies to help our teens.

Some teens might have a genetic predisposition towards anxiety disorders, inheriting a tendency towards heightened emotional sensitivity. This doesn't mean they're destined to develop social anxiety, but it might make them more susceptible to it. It's like having a more sensitive alarm system—their brain might be quicker to perceive social situations as threatening.

Brain chemistry also plays a role. Neurotransmitters like serotonin and dopamine, which regulate mood and emotions, might be imbalanced in individuals with social anxiety. This is why medication that targets these neurotransmitters can sometimes be helpful in treatment.

Environmental influences play a crucial role too. Family dynamics, school experiences, and peer interactions can all contribute to the development of social anxiety. A highly critical home environment, where mistakes are harshly judged, can lead a child to internalize the belief that they're constantly being evaluated negatively by others. Similarly, overprotective parenting might inadvertently send the message that the world is a dangerous place, leading to heightened anxiety in social situations.

Experiences of bullying or social rejection can leave deep emotional scars. A teen who was once mocked for stumbling over their words during a class presentation might develop an intense fear of public speaking. These negative experiences can create a pattern of avoidance, where the teen starts to shy away from similar situations to prevent future embarrassment.

In our digital age, social media's impact on social anxiety can't be overstated. The constant comparison to curated online personas can fuel feelings of inadequacy and anxiety. Teens might feel pressure to present a perfect image online, leading to a disconnect between their online persona and their real-life self. The fear of missing out (FOMO) can drive excessive social media use, paradoxically leading to more anxiety about real-life social interactions.

The instant and often anonymous nature of online communication can make face-to-face interactions feel more daunting. A teen who's used to carefully crafting text messages might feel overwhelmed by the spontaneity required in real-time conversations.

Breaking the cycle of social anxiety involves challenging and reshaping the negative thought patterns that fuel it. Cognitive-behavioral strategies can be particularly effective. These involve identifying negative thoughts that often trigger anxiety, such as "I'll embarrass myself" or "Everyone is judging me," and systematically challenging their validity.

For instance, if your teen thinks, "I always say the wrong thing," you can help them challenge this thought by asking:

- Is this always true? Can you think of times when you've said the right thing?
- What evidence do you have for this thought? Against it?
- If your best friend said they always say the wrong thing, what would you tell them?

By consistently questioning these negative thoughts, teens can start to develop more balanced, realistic perspectives. Over time, this can lead to a reduction in anxiety and an increase in confidence.

Another strategy is gradual exposure. This involves slowly and systematically facing feared social situations, starting with less anxiety-provoking scenarios and working up to more challenging ones. For example, a teen might start by saying hello to one classmate, then progress to having a short conversation, and eventually work up to joining a group activity.

It's important to pair this exposure with relaxation techniques and positive self-talk. Teaching your teen deep breathing exercises or mindfulness practices can give them tools to manage anxiety in the moment. Encouraging them to use affirmations like "I can handle this" or "I am worthy of friendship" can help counteract negative self-talk.

Remember, overcoming social anxiety is a process. It takes time, patience, and consistent effort. But with the right support and strategies, teens can learn to manage their anxiety and develop fulfilling social lives.

Encouraging Social Interaction: Gentle Steps Forward

When it comes to helping teens overcome social anxiety, small steps matter. The idea of attending a party or giving a class presentation might feel overwhelming, but setting micro-goals can lead to significant breakthroughs. It's about building confidence gradually, one small victory at a time.

Start with something as simple as smiling at a classmate or making eye contact. These might seem like tiny actions, but for a teen with social anxiety, they can be significant challenges. Celebrate these small wins—they're the building blocks of social confidence.

Gradually, these small victories can build up to saying hello to a friend, asking a question in class, or joining a group discussion for a few minutes. The key is to set goals that are challenging but achievable. Each success, no matter how small, reinforces the idea that social interactions can be manageable and even enjoyable.

Creating safe social opportunities is crucial. Arrange small gatherings at home where your teen feels comfortable. This could be inviting one or two friends over for a movie night or a gaming session. The familiar environment can help reduce anxiety, allowing your teen to focus on the social interaction itself.

Plan activities that require cooperation but provide enough structure to reduce anxiety. Board games, for instance, offer a structured way to interact while taking the pressure off constant conversation. A pizza-making party combines a fun activity with social interaction, giving your teen something to focus on besides their anxiety.

Extracurricular activities can be a game-changer in developing social skills. Encourage participation in sports, clubs, or arts classes—structured yet informal settings where social interaction is part of the fun. These activities provide natural conversation starters and shared experiences, making it easier to connect with peers.

The key is to encourage activities that genuinely interest your teen, rather than pushing them into popular ones that might feel overwhelming. If your teen loves art, an art club might be less anxiety-provoking than a large team sport. If they're into technology, a robotics club could be a great fit. The shared interest provides common ground, making social interactions feel more natural and less forced.

Practicing social scenarios can also build confidence. Role-play common situations at home, like ordering food at a restaurant, asking a peer about a school assignment, or introducing oneself to a new classmate. This kind of practice can demystify social exchanges and equip your teen with a toolkit of responses they feel prepared to use in real life.

Start with simple scenarios and gradually increase the complexity as your teen's confidence grows. For example, you might start with practicing how to greet someone, then move on to maintaining a short conversation, and eventually work up to more challenging situations like giving a presentation or attending a social event.

Remember, the goal isn't perfection—it's progress. Encourage your teen to focus on their efforts rather than the outcome. Even if an interaction doesn't go as smoothly as they'd hoped, the fact that they tried is a success in itself.

Throughout this process, your support and understanding are crucial. Be patient and empathetic. Acknowledge that what you're asking them to do is challenging. Offer praise for their efforts, not just their successes. Your belief in their ability to overcome their anxiety can be a powerful motivator.

Exercise: Role-Playing for Confidence

## *Objective*

To help teens build confidence and reduce social anxiety through structured role-playing activities.

## Background

Role-playing is an effective tool for managing social anxiety. It provides a safe environment for teens to practice social interactions without the pressure of real-world consequences.

## Instructions

1. Identify Anxiety-Inducing, Realistic Scenarios

   - Discuss with your teen specific social situations that cause anxiety

2. Examples: speaking in class, making small talk, ordering food

3. Assign Roles

   - You play the role of other people in the scenario
   - Your teen practices initiating and maintaining conversations

4. Prepare and Practice

   - Use props to enhance realism (e.g., textbooks, backpacks)
   - Help your teen develop a script or key points to cover
   - Encourage improvisation to handle unexpected turns in conversation

- Example Script

i. Teen: "Hey, I missed yesterday's math class. Could you tell me what the homework assignment was?" Parent (as class-mate): "Sure, we had to do problems 1-15 on page 87." Teen: "Thanks! Do you know when it's due?" Parent: "I think it's due on Friday, but you might want to check with Mr. Johnson to be sure." Teen: "Okay, I'll do that. Thanks for your help!"

5. Provide Constructive Feedback

- Highlight positive aspects (e.g., eye contact, clear voice, good questions)
- Gently suggest improvements (e.g., body language, managing filler words)

6. Encourage Self-Reflection

- Ask your teen to assess their performance
- Discuss how they felt during the role-play

7. Gradually Increase Difficulty

- Introduce more challenging scenarios as confidence grows
- Examples: disagreeing respectfully, joining ongoing conversations

8. Maintain a Supportive Atmosphere

- Keep the mood light and encouraging
- Take breaks if your teen becomes overwhelmed

9. Emphasize Transferable Skills

- Discuss how these skills apply to various life situations
- Examples: job interviews, romantic relationships

As your teen becomes more comfortable with basic scenarios, gradually introduce more challenging situations. This could include role-playing how to respectfully disagree with someone, how to join an ongoing conversation, or how to handle a misunderstanding.

The skills developed through role-playing can extend beyond just managing social anxiety. They're valuable life skills that can help your teen in various aspects of their life.

## Exercise: Building a Social Skills Action Plan

### Objective

To create a personalized, structured plan for teens to develop social confidence and manage anxiety, with parental support.

### Materials

- Notebook or digital device for journaling
- Calendar for tracking progress
- Pens/pencils

### Instructions

1. Initiate Open Conversation

- `Create a safe, non-judgmental space
- Listen actively and empathetically to your teen's concerns about social anxiety

2. Identify Specific Challenges

- List social situations that cause anxiety (e.g., initiating conversations, participating in family gatherings)
- Be as detailed as possible to create a targeted plan

3. Set "SMART Goals" by developing goals that are:

- Specific (e.g., "Say hello to one classmate each day" instead of "Be more social")
- Measurable (e.g., "Participate in class discussions three times a week")
- Achievable (e.g., "Have lunch with one friend" rather than "Attend a large party")
- Relevant (address specific anxiety triggers and align with broader social development)
- Time-bound (e.g., "By the end of the month, I will have initiated three conversations with peers")

4. Establish a Tracking System

- Set up a journal or log (physical or digital)
- Record:

  - Feelings before and after social interactions
  - What went well
  - What was challenging
  - Insights gained

## 5. Conduct Regular Reviews

- Schedule weekly check-ins
- Discuss journal entries supportively
- Identify patterns and areas for improvement
- Adjust goals as needed

## 6. Celebrate Progress

- Acknowledge all successes, no matter how small
- Reinforce positive behavior and boost confidence

## 7. Implement Reward System

- Define milestones
- Choose appropriate rewards (e.g., favorite treats, activities)

## 8. Address Setbacks

- Frame difficulties as learning opportunities
- Discuss how to handle similar situations in the future

## 9. Regularly Revise the Plan

- Be flexible and adapt based on experiences and feedback
- Increase challenge level as confidence grows

## 10. Provide Ongoing Support

- Offer unconditional encouragement and understanding
- Be available to listen without judgment

**Sample Action Plan**

Goal 1: Improve comfort in class discussions

- Week 1-2: Raise hand to answer one question per week
- Week 3-4: Contribute one comment to class discussion per week
- Week 5-6: Ask one question during class per week

Goal 2: Expand social circle

- Month 1: Say hello to one new classmate each week
- Month 2: Have a brief conversation with a classmate once a week
- Month 3: Invite a classmate to study together or have lunch

Goal 3: Increase comfort in group settings

- Step 1: Attend a small group activity (e.g., study group) for 30 minutes
- Step 2: Participate in a structured group activity (e.g., board game night)
- Step 3: Attend a larger social event (e.g., school club meeting) for an hour

It's important to acknowledge that progress may not always be linear. There might be days when your teen takes two steps forward and one step back. That's okay. What matters is the overall trajectory and the resilience they're building along the way.

Also, don't forget to take care of yourself during this process. Supporting a teen with social anxiety can be emotionally taxing.

Make sure you have your own support system and self-care practices in place.

As we wrap up this chapter, remember that navigating social anxiety with your teen isn't about being perfect—it's about being present, understanding, and supportive. It's about creating a safe space for your teen to challenge themselves, make mistakes, and grow.

By implementing these strategies and maintaining open communication, you can help your teen build the confidence and skills they need to thrive socially. It can feel like a lot, but with patience, consistent effort, and lots of love, your teen can overcome social anxiety and develop fulfilling relationships.

Every small step your teen takes is a victory. Every conversation initiated, every class participated in, every social event attended is a testament to their courage and resilience. As they continue to push their boundaries and expand their comfort zone, they're not just overcoming social anxiety—they're building a foundation for a rich, connected life.

In the next chapter, we'll explore more specific strategies for helping teens build confidence in various social situations. We'll look at how to navigate school life, maintain friendships, and handle social media in a healthy way. But for now, take a moment to appreciate how far you've come in understanding and addressing your teen's social anxiety. You're taking important steps to support your child, and that alone is something to be proud of.

THREE

# Communication Skills

In the unfolding story of adolescence, where every interaction can profoundly impact self-awareness and confidence, the mastery of communication skills remains a crucial chapter. Learning how to appropriately express yourself isn't just about crafting well-rounded sentences or mastering the grammar of emotions; it's about building bridges through the art of listening and understanding—the very foundation of all human relationships. As you guide your teen through the complex social landscapes of their world, teaching them the nuances of effective communication becomes essential. It's about equipping them with the tools not just to speak, but more importantly, to listen, empathize, understand, and transform their interactions into meaningful exchanges.

### Listening with Empathy: The First Step to Understanding

Listening is a crucial skill for building strong relationships and understanding others. For teenagers, learning to listen with empathy can make a big difference in how they connect with people and handle social situations. By mastering active listening, your teen can improve their friendships, family relationships, and even how they handle disagreements. Good listening isn't just about hearing words—it's about understanding feelings and showing others that they matter.

While both empathy and sympathy involve responses to the feelings and experiences of others, they differ significantly in their depth and effectiveness. Empathy involves putting yourself in another person's shoes, understanding their feelings and perspectives as if they were your own. In contrast, sympathy is more about feeling sorry for someone's difficulties, which can sometimes create a sense of distance. You can help your teen develop empathy by discussing various scenarios and asking how they would feel in that situation, encouraging them to go beyond surface emotions to a more nuanced understanding of others' experiences.

Active listening is the cornerstone of effective communication, allowing you to fully engage with others' words and meaning. It involves fully concentrating, understanding, responding, and then remembering what is being said. Here are some techniques that can improve your teen's active listening skills:

- Maintaining eye contact: Encourage them to maintain eye contact, which shows interest and respect for the speaker and helps to focus on what's being said.
- Paraphrasing and summarizing: Teach them the subtle art of paraphrasing and summarizing what they've heard. This not only demonstrates that they are paying attention but also helps them grasp the message on a deeper level.
- Asking thoughtful questions: You might also introduce the practice of asking thoughtful questions, which shows

engagement and encourages further discussion, making the speaker feel valued and heard.

Modeling active listening in your daily interactions can serve as a powerful teaching tool for your teen. Demonstrate empathy by listening attentively to their concerns without interrupting, showing understanding, and responding appropriately. Discuss the importance of listening not just to respond, but to understand. Turn everyday interactions into opportunities for connection and learning. Additionally, setting up family discussions where everyone gets a chance to speak and be heard can reinforce these skills. During these sessions, emphasize the importance of patience and respect for the speaker, qualities that are essential for active listening.

Empathetic listening can often serve as a bridge over troubled waters of conflict. By genuinely trying to see each party's perspective and emotions, it becomes easier to find solutions that are acceptable to all involved. Teach your teen that in the midst of disagreement, it's crucial to step back and listen with the intent to understand, not to counter-argue. This approach doesn't just de-escalate conflicts; it also strengthens relationships by fostering mutual respect and understanding. Discuss situations at home where empathetic listening led to peaceful resolutions, and encourage your teen to apply these lessons in their own interactions.

### Expressing Themselves: Encouraging Open Dialogue

Fostering an environment where your teen feels confident and comfortable expressing themselves is crucial for their emotional and social development. One of the primary components of such an environment is helping teens build a robust vocabulary for their emotions. Often, teens might feel a surge of emotions but lack the precise words to express them, leading to frustration or misunderstanding. Start by introducing more nuanced emotional words during your conversations. For instance, instead of using broad terms like 'happy' or 'sad', encourage descriptions like 'elated', 'content', 'melancholy', or 'dejected'. You can facilitate this development by creating an 'emotion chart' with words and expressions describing various emotions and placing it somewhere visible in your home. When discussing how events made you or them feel, regularly refer to this chart, which not only expands their emotional vocabulary but also normalizes the discussion of feelings in everyday conversations. This practice helps teens articulate their emotions more accurately, making it easier for them to communicate their inner experiences and needs.

Creating a safe space for sharing is equally essential to encouraging open dialogue. This space is both physical and emotional; it requires an atmosphere where teens know that their feelings and thoughts are respected and valued. Establish specific times and settings that are dedicated to sharing and listening – perhaps a weekly 'family meeting' or a daily chat over dinner where each family member can discuss their day and anything on their mind. During these times, it's crucial to ensure that the environment is free from distractions like cell phones or televisions.

When your teen shares their thoughts, show genuine interest and refrain from judgment or immediate correction. Instead, respond with empathy and validation, demonstrating that you appreciate their willingness to share and that their feelings are important. This consistent practice not only makes your teen feel valued but also teaches them that it's safe to offer their opinions and feelings, a lesson they will carry into other relationships.

Teaching the use of 'I' statements is another powerful tool for helping teens express themselves constructively. These statements focus on the speaker's feelings rather than blaming or criticizing others, which can help prevent conversations from escalating into conflicts. For example, instead of saying, "You never listen to me," a more constructive statement would be, "I feel ignored when I talk and others don't seem to listen." This shift reduces defensiveness in others and empowers the speaker to focus on what they can control – how they express their feelings. Role-play various scenarios with your teen where 'I' statements would be useful. Start with simple, low-stakes situations like expressing disappointment over a canceled plan, and gradually progress to more challenging emotional expressions like feeling hurt by a friend's actions. This gradual escalation allows your teen to become comfortable using 'I' statements in various contexts, enhancing their ability to communicate both assertively and empathetically.

Role-playing, a versatile tool that your teen is already familiar with from previous exercises, can be extended to practice expressing emotions and thoughts constructively. Set up scenarios that your teen is likely to encounter, such as dealing with a misunderstanding with a friend or asking a teacher for help. In these role-plays, encourage your teen to use the emotional vocabulary they've developed and to utilize 'I' statements to express their feelings. Provide feedback, focusing on their choice of words, tone, and body language, ensuring that all elements contribute to a thoughtful and clear expression of their views and emotions.

Exercise: Constructive Expression Role-Play

### *Objective*

To practice expressing emotions and thoughts constructively using role-play scenarios.

### Materials

- List of potential scenarios (provided below)
- Emotion vocabulary chart
- Notepad for feedback

### Instructions

1. Choose a scenario from the list or create one that's relevant to your teen's experiences.

2. Assign roles: one person plays the teen, the other plays the second character in the scenario.

3. Before starting, remind your teen to:

- Use the emotional vocabulary they've learned
- Utilize 'I' statements to express feelings
- Pay attention to tone of voice and body language

4. Act out the scenario for 3-5 minutes.

5. After the role-play, provide feedback:

- Highlight effective use of emotional vocabulary
- Point out successful 'I' statements
- Discuss tone of voice and body language

- Suggest areas for improvement

6. Switch roles and try another scenario.

**Potential Scenarios**

1. Explaining to a friend why you're upset about a misunderstanding
2. Asking a teacher for help with a difficult assignment
3. Discussing a curfew extension with a parent
4. Addressing a teammate who isn't pulling their weight on a group project
5. Talking to a sibling about respecting personal space

**Tips for Effective Feedback**

- Be specific about what worked well
- Offer constructive suggestions for improvement
- Encourage self-reflection: "How do you think that went?"

**Practice Schedule**

- Aim to do 2-3 role-plays per week
- Gradually increase the complexity of scenarios
- Encourage your teen to apply these skills in daily life

**Reflection**

After several practice sessions, discuss with your teen:

- How has their comfort level with expressing emotions changed?

- What differences have they noticed in their real-life interactions?
- Which aspects of constructive expression still feel challenging?

This exercise provides your teen with a safe space to experiment with and refine their communication style, which can boost their confidence in handling similar situations in real life. As these practices become more integrated into their daily habits, your teen will find it increasingly natural to open up and express themselves in ways that foster understanding and respect, thus significantly enhancing their relationships.

## Non-Verbal Communication: Reading and Responding to Cues

Navigating the nuanced world of non-verbal communication is akin to understanding a silent language that speaks volumes. Body language, facial expressions, and tone of voice are crucial components of this language, each adding layers of meaning to the words spoken. When a teen learns to interpret these cues accurately, it enhances their ability to connect with others, understand unspoken emotions, and respond more empathetically. For instance, a slumped posture might indicate sadness or defeat, while crossed arms could suggest defensiveness or discomfort. Facial expressions can convey a myriad of emotions from joy to sorrow, and even subtle changes can significantly alter the message's impact. Tone of voice, too, plays a vital role—it can communicate sarcasm, anger, affection, or sincerity, often overriding the literal meaning of the spoken words.

Teaching your teen to pay attention to these silent signals requires more than just pointing them out; it involves nurturing observation skills and empathy. Observational skills can be enhanced through games like watching a muted video clip and trying to deduce the context and emotions based solely on body language and facial expressions. Discuss these observations with your teen, sharing insights on what you each perceive and why. This exercise not only sharpens their ability to pick up on non-verbal cues but also encourages them to pay attention to details that might otherwise be overlooked.

The congruence between what is said and how it's said—verbal and non-verbal alignment—is equally crucial. Inconsistencies between the two can lead to confusion and mistrust. For example, if someone says they're fine, but their voice is flat and their shoulders are slumped, non-verbal signals might suggest otherwise. Helping your teen understand this congruence involves analyzing real-life interactions or role-playing exercises where they practice aligning their verbal messages with their non-verbal signals. This could include practicing maintaining an open posture while communicating or ensuring that their facial expression matches the emotion they're expressing. These practices help teens become more authentic communicators and more perceptive listeners, attuned to the true content of what's being communicated.

In the realm of digital interactions, the transmission and interpretation of non-verbal cues undergo a transformation. While digital platforms strip away much of body language and tone, they often leave room for different types of non-verbal communication, such as the timing of responses, the use of emojis, or the choice of words and punctuation—consider a text message that ends in a period versus an exclamation point.

These nuances can drastically alter the perceived tone and intent behind digital communications. Misinterpretations are common without facial expressions and vocal tone, leading to misunderstandings that can escalate into unnecessary conflicts.

To navigate this, discuss with your teen the importance of clarity in their digital communications. Encourage them to consider how their messages might be perceived and to consider adding clarifying comments or questions if a message could be interpreted ambiguously. Also, stress the importance of discussing sensitive topics in person whenever possible, as this allows for a more complete exchange of verbal and non-verbal signals, reducing the likelihood of misunderstandings.

By fostering an awareness and understanding of non-verbal communication, you empower your teen not only to express themselves more effectively but also to enhance their interpretations of others' communications, both in-person and online. This skill set is crucial as it ensures their growth into empathetic, perceptive individuals capable of navigating complex social landscapes with confidence and understanding.

### The Art of Small Talk: Practice Makes Perfect

Small talk is often dismissed as mere filler conversation, but it actually plays a significant role in human interaction. For teenagers, mastering small talk is crucial for building deeper relationships and creating new opportunities. It's like getting warmed up before soccer practice, setting the stage for a more detailed conversation. Small talk helps teens connect with others and gradually move on to more substantial topics. By engaging in these seemingly trivial exchanges, teens learn to navigate conversations, understand their peers' interests, and find common ground for deeper connections.

To engage in small talk effectively, start with topics that are relatable and non-controversial. Discuss hobbies, books, movies, or observations about shared experiences. Encourage your teen to ask simple questions like, "Have you read any good books lately?" or "What did you think of the game last night?" Guide them towards open-ended questions that require more than a yes or no answer, which can help the conversation flow more naturally and reveal more about the interests and personalities of those they're engaging with. To make small talk more engaging, stress the importance of showing genuine interest in the other person's opinions and experiences.

Exercise: Small Talk Role-Play

### Objective

To practice small talk skills in a safe environment before applying them in real-world situations.

### Materials

- List of scenario prompts (provided below)
- Timer
- Notepad for feedback

### Instructions

1. Choose a scenario from the list or create one relevant to your teen's life.
2. Set the scene briefly, describing the context and any relevant details.
3. Assign roles: Parent plays a new acquaintance, teen plays themselves.
4. Set a timer for 3-5 minutes and begin the role-play.
5. After the timer ends, spend 5 minutes on feedback and discussion.

6. Switch roles or try a new scenario, aiming for 3-4 practice sessions.

**Scenario Prompts**

1. Meeting a new student at a school club meeting
2. Talking to a neighbor at a community barbecue
3. Striking up a conversation with a classmate before a sports match
4. Chatting with a friend's cousin at a birthday party
5. Making small talk with a store clerk while shopping

**During the role-play, encourage your teen to:**

- Use open-ended questions
- Show genuine interest in responses
- Maintain appropriate eye contact
- Use friendly body language

**Feedback Guidelines**

- Start with positive observations
- Offer specific, constructive suggestions
- Ask your teen for their own thoughts on the interaction

Sample Feedback: "I liked how you asked about their hobbies. Next time, try following up on their answer with another question to show more interest."

**Discussion Points**

- What felt natural or challenging about the conversation?
- How might this scenario play out differently in real life?

- What strategies could help in moments of awkward silence?

**Tips**

- Gradually increase the difficulty of scenarios
- Encourage your teen to initiate these practices when they feel ready
- Remind them that it's okay to make mistakes – that's part of learning

Feedback is crucial here; provide gentle guidance on how they can improve their conversational skills, such as using more open-ended questions, showing more interest in the responses they receive, or even how to better use their body language to convey engagement and openness.

Addressing the potential awkwardness of conversations—entering, maintaining, or leaving them—can be a significant concern for teens, who may feel anxious about the possibility of social missteps. Teach your teen that entering a conversation can be as simple as a smile and a greeting, followed by a relevant observation or question that relates to the context or situation. Maintaining the conversation can involve active listening, nodding, or asking follow-up questions based on what the other person says. Exiting a conversation gracefully can be done with polite phrases that signal a conclusion without abruptness, such as "It was great talking with you" or "I hope to hear more about it later." Handling silent moments doesn't have to be daunting; they can be viewed as natural parts of a conversation where both parties are processing the discussion or considering what to say next. Encourage your teen to use pauses as an opportunity to introduce a new topic or ask another question, seamlessly continuing the flow of conversation.

By incorporating these techniques into their social toolkit, your teen can transform small talk from a mere exchange of pleasantries into a powerful component of their communication skills repertoire. Such skills not only enhance their daily interactions but also boost their confidence in managing and nurturing the relationships they will encounter throughout their lives.

### Conflict Resolution: Navigating Disagreements Constructively

Conflict is an inevitable part of human interaction, and for teenagers navigating complex social networks, learning to handle disagreements constructively is a crucial life skill. The first step in effective conflict resolution is identifying the root of conflicts. Often, what appears to be the cause of a disagreement is merely a symptom of a deeper issue. Teach your teen to look beyond surface-level arguments and consider underlying emotions, needs, or misunderstandings that might be fueling the conflict. Encourage them to ask themselves and others involved questions like, "What's really bothering me/you about this situation?" or "What need isn't being met here?" This deeper understanding can pave the way for more meaningful resolutions.

When it comes to communicating during conflicts, maintaining calm and being clear are key. Teach your teen strategies for staying composed in heated moments, such as taking deep breaths, calling for a short break if emotions are running high, or using "I" statements to express feelings without accusation. Emphasize the importance of listening actively to the other person's perspective, even if they disagree. Encourage them to paraphrase what they've heard to ensure understanding and show that they're genuinely trying to see the other person's point of view.

Finding common ground is often the bridge to resolution in conflicts. Guide your teen to look for shared values, goals, or interests that can serve as a foundation for working together towards a solution. This might involve asking questions like, "What do we both want to achieve here?" or "Can we agree on the importance of [shared value]?" By focusing on areas of agreement, even small ones, teens can build momentum towards resolving larger disagreements.

Role-playing is an excellent tool for practicing conflict resolution skills in a safe environment. Set up scenarios that mimic real-life conflicts your teen might encounter, such as disagreements with friends, siblings, or even teachers. Take turns playing different roles, allowing your teen to practice both expressing their own needs and listening to others. After each role-play, discuss what went well and what could be improved. Here's an example scenario to get started:

Scenario: Your teen and their friend have a group project due, but they disagree on how to approach it.

Teen: "I think we should focus on creating a visual presentation. It'll be more engaging." Parent (as friend): "But I think a written report would be more thorough and get us a better grade." Teen: "I understand you're concerned about our grade. That's important to me too. Maybe we could find a way to combine both approaches?" Parent: "That's a good point. What if we do a written report but include some visual elements to make it more engaging?" Teen: "I like that idea. We could play to both our strengths that way."

This example demonstrates looking for common ground (concern about grades), expressing understanding of the other's perspective, and working together to find a solution that addresses both parties' concerns.

Let's try it out.

## Exercise: Conflict Resolution Role-Play

### *Objective*

To practice handling disagreements constructively through impro-vised scenarios.

### Materials

- Timer
- Notebook and pen for observer

### Instructions

1. Divide into groups of three: two participants and one observer.

2. The participants will create their own conflict scenario based on common teen experiences. Spend 2-3 minutes brainstorming a realistic situation.

3. Assign roles based on the scenario they've created. The observer will take notes and time the interaction.

4. Role-play the scenario for 5-7 minutes, focusing on:

- Identifying the root of the conflict
- Using "I" statements
- Active listening
- Finding common ground
- Proposing solutions

5. After the role-play, spend 5 minutes discussing:

- What went well?
- What could have been handled differently?
- How did it feel to be in each role?

6. Switch roles and create a new scenario to repeat the process.

## Guidelines for Creating Scenarios

Encourage participants to think of common conflicts teens might face, such as:

- Disagreements with parents about rules or privileges
- Conflicts with friends over misunderstandings or differing opinions
- Issues with teachers or coaches about grades, playing time, or expectations
- Sibling rivalries or disputes

## Guidelines for Participants

- Stay in character
- Be open to compromise
- Listen to understand, not just to respond
- Focus on the issue, not personal attacks

## Guidelines for Observer

- Note specific phrases or actions that escalate or de-escalate the conflict
- Watch for non-verbal cues
- Time the interaction
- Prepare constructive feedback

**Reflection**

After completing 2-3 rounds, gather as a larger group to discuss:

- Common challenges in resolving conflicts
- Effective strategies observed
- How these skills can be applied in real-life situations

This exercise allows teens to practice conflict resolution in a safe environment, helping them develop crucial communication and problem-solving skills they can use in various real-life situations. By creating their own scenarios, they can address conflicts that feel most relevant and realistic to their lives.

### Bonus: Reflective Journaling Prompt

Consider incorporating a reflective journaling exercise where, after each role-play session, your teen writes about the experience. They should note what techniques worked, how they felt during the conflict, and what they might do differently next time. This reflection can deepen their understanding of conflict dynamics and their personal conflict resolution style, fostering ongoing learning and improvement in their communication skills.

To bridge the gap between practice and real-life application, encourage your teen to identify one upcoming social situation where they can apply these skills in the short term, such as a group project at school or a family gathering. For a long-term approach, suggest they keep a "real-life authenticity journal" where they document instances of staying true to themselves in social situations, reflecting on their successes and areas for improvement. This ongoing practice will help solidify their ability to navigate social pressures authentically in various real-world contexts.

As we close this chapter and look ahead, the skills your teen has begun to develop will be put into action as we explore more about building confidence and leadership in the following chapters. These next steps are not just about avoiding or managing conflicts, but about leading by example and setting a tone that promotes understanding and respect in all interactions.

# FOUR

# Emotional Intelligence

During adolescence, emotions can feel incredibly intense and overwhelming for both teens and parents. Emotional Intelligence (EI) provides a valuable set of skills to not just survive these years, but to thrive. Unlike IQ, which remains relatively stable, emotional intelligence is a dynamic set of abilities that influence how well we perceive, understand, and manage emotions in ourselves and others. These skills, including self-awareness, self-regulation, motivation, empathy, and social relationships, are essential tools that can guide your teen through the complexities of their emotional experiences. By fostering emotional intelligence, you're providing your teen with the means to navigate their emotional world, enhancing their ability to engage with others, make decisions, and pursue their goals with confidence and clarity.

## Recognizing Emotions: The Basics of Emotional Intelligence

At its core, emotional intelligence is the ability to recognize, understand, and manage one's own emotions, as well as the ability

to handle interpersonal relationships judiciously and empathetically. This multifaceted skill set is built on five key areas:

1. Self-awareness: The ability to recognize and understand
   your own emotions
2. Self-regulation: The ability to manage, control, and adapt
   your emotions, behavior, and responses to situations
3. Motivation: The drive to pursue goals with energy and
   persistence
4. Empathy: The ability to understand, recognize, and
   consider others' feelings, especially when making decisions
5. Social skills: The ability to manage relationships to move
   people in desired directions, whether in leading,
   negotiating, or working as part of a team

These components work synergistically to enable individuals to
recognize, connect with, and learn from their own and others'
emotions, which is crucial not only for personal satisfaction but
also for success in various aspects of life.

To instill emotional awareness in your teen, start with simple exercises that encourage them to tune into their emotions. One effective tool is the 'Emotion Meter' exercise, where you ask your teen
to imagine their emotional state as a meter running from 'very
low' to 'very high'. Throughout the day, at random moments, ask
them to 'check' this meter and identify what emotion they're
feeling and its intensity. This exercise not only helps them become
more aware of their emotional fluctuations but also helps them
recognize what events or interactions trigger different emotions.
Another useful practice is mindfulness meditation, focusing on
breathing and bodily sensations. This can help teens become more
attuned to their emotional states as they arise.

The ability to accurately identify emotions is a crucial component of emotional intelligence and can significantly improve emotional regulation. When teens can pinpoint their emotions, they're better equipped to address them effectively. For instance, recognizing the difference between feeling 'irritated' and 'angry' can lead to more appropriate responses and interactions with others. Encourage your teen to expand their emotional vocabulary beyond basic labels like "sad" or "happy." Introduce them to more nuanced terms like 'melancholy', 'anxious', or 'content', which can provide a clearer understanding of their emotional state. This practice not only improves their self-awareness but also enhances their communication with others, as they can express their feelings more accurately.

Emotional intelligence has a significant and measurable impact on success. Research shows that individuals with high EI have better mental health, job performance, and leadership skills. Studies suggest that emotional intelligence accounts for nearly 90% of what sets high performers apart from peers with similar technical skills and knowledge (Cavaness et al., 2020). When it comes to academics, teens with higher emotional intelligence are better equipped to handle academic pressures and interactions with peers and teachers; they also tend to have better conflict resolution skills and a more positive attitude towards school. Teaching your teen about the importance of emotional intelligence for real-world success can motivate them to consistently develop and apply these skills.

Exercise: Emotion Word of the Week

### Objective

To expand your teen's emotional vocabulary and enhance their ability to identify and express complex emotions.

### Materials

- Index cards or small pieces of paper
- Pen or marker
- Tape or magnets (for posting on the fridge)
- List of complex emotion words (provided below)

### Instructions

1. At the beginning of each week, choose a new emotion word from the list.

2. Write the word and its definition on an index card or piece of paper.

3. Post the card in a visible place, such as the refrigerator or family bulletin board.

4. During a family meal or dedicated time, introduce the word:

- Read the definition aloud
- Discuss situations where someone might feel this emotion
- Share personal experiences related to the emotion, if comfortable

5. Challenge family members to use the word throughout the week when describing their feelings.

6. At the end of the week, have a brief discussion:

- How often did family members use or notice the emotion?
- Did using a more specific word help in understanding or expressing feelings?

7. Keep the used cards in a visible place to review and reinforce learning.

Sample Emotion Words:

- Melancholy
- Exhilarated
- Apprehensive
- Indignant
- Wistful
- Ambivalent
- Nostalgic
- Vulnerable
- Jubilant
- Despondent

**Tips**

- Encourage your teen to journal about times they experience the emotion of the week.
- Use the words in everyday conversations to model their usage.
- Consider creating a family game where points are earned for appropriately using the word of the week.

By focusing intently on developing your teen's emotional intelligence, you are setting them up not just for academic and professional success, but for a richer, more understanding, and empathetic life. These skills enable teens to navigate their emotional world with finesse, making them better students and friends, as well as, ultimately, more compassionate and effective leaders.

## Managing Emotions: Strategies for Self-Regulation

In navigating the emotional complexity of the teenage years, self-regulation stands out as a critical skill that allows individuals to maintain control over their feelings and reactions, thus fostering a healthier emotional life. This ability to manage one's emotions isn't innate; rather, it's cultivated through consistent practice and the application of specific techniques that can be integrated into daily life. One of the most effective of these strategies is deep breathing, which has been shown to reduce stress and promote calmness by slowing the heart rate and providing the brain with the oxygen it needs to achieve a state of calm. Encourage your teen to practice deep breathing by inhaling slowly to a count of four, holding the breath for a count of four, then exhaling to a count of four. This technique can be particularly useful in moments of high stress or anxiety, providing them with a tool that's always available to them, no matter where they are or what situation they're in.

Mindfulness, another powerful tool for emotional regulation, involves maintaining a moment-by-moment awareness of our thoughts, feelings, bodily sensations, and surrounding environment. This practice helps teens to observe their emotions without judgment, recognizing them as temporary states that don't define their identity or capabilities. You can encourage your teen to practice mindfulness through simple exercises such as mindful walking, where the focus is on the sensation of moving and touching the ground, or mindful eating, which involves paying close attention to the eating experience and the textures, flavors, and smells of the food. These practices help to anchor them in the present moment, providing a respite from the stress of past memories or future anxieties.

Positive self-talk is another essential component of self-regulation, influencing the emotional response to various situations. Negative self-talk can spiral into emotional distress, while positive self-talk can empower and bring clarity. Encourage your teen to recognize negative thought patterns and replace them with positive affirmations. For instance, instead of thinking, "I can't handle this," they can reframe it as, "I can handle this situation step by step." Over time, this shift in internal dialogue can significantly alter their emotional landscape, changing how they perceive and react to challenges.

Maintaining emotional balance often directly correlates with how well we take care of our physical health. Regular exercise, adequate sleep, and healthy eating habits are fundamental elements that contribute significantly to emotional well-being. Physical activity, for instance, isn't just about staying in shape; it's a powerful mood enhancer and anxiety reducer. Encourage your teen to find a form of exercise they enjoy, whether it's dancing, skateboarding, or playing soccer. The key is consistency and enjoyment, which will make it more likely that they'll stick with it.

Sleep also plays a crucial role in emotional regulation. Lack of sleep can make teens more prone to emotional instability, irritability, and stress. Help your teen establish a healthy sleep routine by encouraging a consistent bedtime and creating a pre-sleep ritual that avoids screens and incorporates calming activities like reading or listening to soothing music. Dietary habits also influence mood and energy levels. Diets high in processed foods and sugars can exacerbate feelings of lethargy and depression, while a balanced diet rich in vegetables, fruits, and whole grains can improve energy and emotional resilience. Discuss these connections with your teen and involve them in making better food choices; perhaps plan and cook meals together to make this practice more engaging and educational.

Helping your teen set and maintain healthy emotional boundaries is crucial for their self-esteem and emotional well-being. These boundaries help them define what they're comfortable with and how they want to be treated by others. Encourage your teen to listen to their feelings and recognize when a situation or person is making them uncomfortable. Discuss scenarios where they might need to assert their boundaries, such as when someone asks them to do something they're not comfortable with or when they need personal space. Role-playing can be a useful tool here, helping them practice how to assert themselves in a respectful and confident manner. It's important they understand that saying no is a right, not a privilege, and that setting boundaries is a sign of self-respect, not selfishness.

The ability to pause and choose how to respond to a situation is a sophisticated skill that lies at the heart of emotional intelligence. This practice involves shifting from being reactive—acting on immediate emotional impulses—to being responsive—taking a moment to consider the best course of action. Encourage your teen to develop the habit of pausing when they feel emotionally triggered. This pause can be as simple as taking three deep breaths to give them time to consider how best to respond. During this time, they can evaluate whether their immediate reaction is likely to lead to a positive outcome or whether there might be a better way to handle the situation. This practice not only prevents regrettable actions made in the heat of the moment but also empowers your teen to approach challenges in a more thoughtful and effective manner.

By incorporating these strategies and practices into their daily life, your teen can develop powerful self-regulation skills that will serve them well through adolescence and beyond. These skills are fundamental to self-mastery, fostering a sense of control and resilience that will help them navigate the complex emotional landscapes of their teenage years and prepare them for the adult world.

## Empathy: Walking in Someone Else's Shoes

As we discussed earlier in Chapter 3, empathy is a crucial skill for effective communication and building relationships. In the context of emotional intelligence, empathy takes on an even more significant role. It's not just about understanding others' feelings, but also using that understanding to navigate social situations more effectively.

Empathy and active listening, which we explored in depth previously, are fundamental to developing high emotional intelligence. They allow teens to pick up on subtle emotional cues, respond appropriately to others' feelings, and build stronger, more meaningful connections. By honing these skills, teens can enhance their overall emotional intelligence, leading to better social outcomes and personal growth.

The impact of empathy on relationships cannot be overstated. It serves as a powerful bridge between individuals, fostering a culture of trust and openness. When your teen learns to empathize, they're not just understanding another person's situation; they're also validating their feelings. This validation can be incredibly affirming, strengthening the bonds between individuals. It encourages a reciprocal flow of openness and trust that can transform relationships. For instance, when a friend or family member is going through a difficult time, your teen's ability to empathize allows them to offer genuine support and understanding, which can be crucial for the other person's emotional well-being. In turn, this builds a relationship based on mutual respect and understanding, qualities that are essential for lasting connections.

To enhance empathy, consider incorporating practices into your teen's routine that foster perspective-taking and emotional understanding. Volunteer work is an excellent way for teens to experience different situations that challenge their viewpoints and evoke empathy. Whether it's helping at a local shelter, assisting in community clean-up efforts, or participating in programs for underprivileged groups, these activities can open their eyes to the realities of different lives. Such experiences not only cultivate a deeper understanding of societal issues but also inspire a profound sense of empathy for individuals from diverse backgrounds.

## Exercise: Empathy Through Community Engagement

### *Objective*

To develop empathy and broaden perspectives through hands-on volunteer experiences.

### Materials

- List of local volunteer opportunities
- Calendar for planning
- Journal or notebook

### Instructions

1. Research and Exploration (1-2 weeks):

- Together with your teen, research local volunteer opportunities.
- Look for diverse options such as:

  - Animal shelters
  - Food banks
  - Community clean-up projects
  - Senior centers
  - Youth mentoring programs
  - Homeless shelters

2. Selection and Planning:

- Have your teen choose 2-3 different volunteer activities.
- Schedule these activities over the course of 1-3 months.
- Discuss expectations and any concerns before each activity.

3. Engagement:

- Participate in the chosen volunteer activities together.
- Encourage your teen to interact with people they meet and ask questions.

4. Reflection: After each volunteer experience, engage in a reflection session:

- What surprised you about this experience?
- How did it make you feel?
- Did you meet anyone whose story impacted you? How?
- How has this changed your perspective on [relevant issue]?

5. Journaling:

- Have your teen write about their experiences in a journal.
- Prompt them to describe not just what they did, but how it affected them emotionally.

6. Follow-up Discussion:

- After completing all planned activities, have a family discussion about the overall experience.
- Explore how these experiences have influenced your teen's understanding of others and their empathy levels.

7. Continued Engagement:

- Based on your teen's interests and reflections, consider committing to regular volunteer work in one area.

**Tips**

- Lead by example; share your own reflections and emotional responses.
- Encourage your teen to step out of their comfort zone, but be supportive if they find certain experiences challenging.
- Use these experiences as springboards for discussions about social issues, inequality, and the importance of community support.

Additionally, exploring diverse perspectives is another enriching exercise. This can be achieved through family discussions about current events, books, or movies that explore complex human emotions and situations. Encourage your teen to share their thoughts and feelings about the characters or situations, and explore how they might feel in similar circumstances. These conversations can be instrumental in fostering a well-rounded, empathetic approach to differing viewpoints.

In the digital world, empathy presents unique challenges. Often, the nuances of face-to-face interaction, such as tone of voice and body language, are lost in online communication, making it harder to perceive and convey empathy. This can lead to misunderstandings or a perceived lack of concern. To help your teen navigate these challenges, discuss the importance of being mindful of how their words might be interpreted without the benefit of non-verbal cues. Encourage them to use empathetic language that reflects thoughtfulness and understanding, as well as to ask clarifying questions to ensure they've accurately perceived others' messages. Additionally, practicing empathy online can involve acknowledging others' emotions explicitly and offering support through thoughtful comments or messages. These practices can make a significant difference in fostering meaningful connections, even through digital mediums. Importantly, developing these digital empathy skills directly enhances emotional intelligence by improving one's ability to recognize, understand, and respond to emotions in various contexts, building upon the foundational empathy concepts discussed in Chapter 3.

By teaching your teen to cultivate empathy, both offline and online, you equip them with the ability to understand and connect with others deeply, enhancing their interpersonal relationships and boosting their emotional intelligence. This skill set not only aids their personal and social interactions but also prepares them to engage with the world from a more compassionate and comprehensive perspective.

### Resilience: Bouncing Back from Social Setbacks

Resilience, often envisioned as the psychological armor against the slings and arrows of outrageous fortune, is fundamentally about more than just enduring; it's about adapting and thriving in the face of adversity. In the context of social interactions, particularly during the tumultuous years of adolescence, resilience is the ability to recover from setbacks, learn from failure, and move forward with a more refined understanding and renewed vigor. This capacity is especially critical for teenagers, who often face a myriad of social challenges, from navigating complex friendship dynamics to dealing with rejection or bullying. Understanding and cultivating resilience can transform these potentially traumatic experiences into powerful opportunities for growth and learning.

Fostering a resilient mindset is a proactive approach that involves reframing challenges as catalysts for growth. This mindset, rooted in what psychologist Carol Dweck terms a "growth mindset," contrasts sharply with a "fixed mindset," which views abilities and intelligence as static and sees challenges as threats (Dweck, 2012). Encourage your teen to view setbacks as opportunities to expand their skills and gain new insights. For example, if they face rejection from a group, rather than interpreting it as a personal failure, guide them to see it as a chance to explore new social circles and develop broader interests. This perspective not only mitigates the pain associated with the experience but also propels them towards self-discovery and personal growth.

To nurture this mindset, regular discussions about the nature of learning and growth can be incredibly beneficial. Highlight stories of individuals who have overcome significant social setbacks to achieve remarkable personal and professional success. These narratives can serve as powerful reminders that current difficulties do not define future outcomes, and that persistence and resilience can lead to unexpected and fulfilling paths. Additionally, focusing on intrinsic rather than extrinsic rewards can reinforce the value of self-improvement. Encourage your teen to set goals related to acquiring new skills or expanding knowledge in areas of interest, rather than goals solely tied to social acceptance or status. This shift in focus can lessen the sting of social challenges and reframe their purpose from gaining external validation to enhancing personal growth.

### Exercise: Building Your Personal Resilience Toolkit

*Objective*

To create a personalized set of coping strategies for your teen to manage stress, disappointment, and failure.

**Materials**

- Notebook or journal
- Pens or pencils
- Art supplies (optional)
- Yoga mat or comfortable space for relaxation exercises

**Instructions**

1. Journaling for Reflection (15-20 minutes daily)

- Dedicate a notebook specifically for resilience journaling.
- Each day, have your teen write about:
- A challenge they faced
- How they felt during and after
- What they learned from the experience
- How they might apply this lesson in the future

- At the end of each week, sit with your teen and review their entries to identify patterns in their responses to challenges.

2. Stress-Relief Activity Menu (One-time setup, then daily practice)

- Sit down with your teen and create a list of 5-10 activities that help them relax and reduce stress. Examples might include:

  - Deep breathing exercises
  - Drawing or coloring
  - Listening to calming music
  - Taking a nature walk
  - Practicing yoga or stretching

- Encourage your teen to engage in at least one of these activities daily, especially during stressful times. Consider joining them occasionally to model the importance of stress management.

3. Positive Affirmation Creation (Weekly)

- Each week, work with your teen to create a new positive affirmation based on a challenge they're facing or a strength they want to reinforce.
- Help them write it down and place it somewhere visible in their room.
- Encourage them to repeat the affirmation to themselves several times a day, especially when feeling stressed or discouraged.

4. Problem-Solving Practice (As needed)

When your teen faces a difficult situation, guide them through these steps: a) Help them write down the problem. b) Brainstorm together to list at least three possible solutions. c) Discuss the pros and cons of each solution. d) Support them in choosing one to implement. e) After implementing, reflect together on the outcome and encourage them to journal about it.

5. Gratitude Log (Daily)

- Introduce the concept of a gratitude journal to your teen.
- Encourage them to write down three things they're grateful for each day.
- Challenge them to find new things to appreciate, especially on difficult days.
- Consider sharing your own gratitudes at dinner time to make it a family activity.

6. Resilience Role Model Research (Monthly)

- Suggest that your teen research someone who has shown great resilience in the face of adversity.
- Ask them to write a short summary of the person's story and what they find inspiring about their resilience.
- Discuss their findings together, drawing parallels to your teen's life where appropriate.

7. Toolkit Review and Update (Monthly)

- At the end of each month, review your teen's journal entries and activities together.
- Discuss what strategies worked best for them.

- Help them adjust their toolkit as needed, adding new techniques or modifying existing ones.

Remember to approach these activities with patience and support. Your involvement can greatly enhance your teen's resilience-building journey and strengthen your relationship.

The resilience toolkit contains essential tools for managing particularly difficult times for handling stress, disappointment, and failure. Techniques such as journaling can provide a safe outlet for emotional expression and reflection. Encourage your teen to write about their experiences and feelings, focusing on what they learned from each situation and how they can apply these lessons in the future. This practice aids in processing emotions and, moreover, in identifying patterns in how they respond to challenges, which can be insightful for personal growth. Additionally, engaging in activities that promote relaxation and stress relief, such as yoga or creative arts, can provide a healthy escape from social stressors, offering space and energy to approach problems with a clearer mind.

Learning from failure is perhaps the most crucial aspect of developing resilience. It involves shifting the narrative from viewing failure as a negative endpoint to seeing it as an essential part of the growth process. This shift requires a supportive environment where mistakes are tolerated, as well as regular steps in the direction of learning and adapting. When your teen experiences a social setback, help them analyze the situation to understand what factors were within their control and what lessons could be gleaned. Was it a matter of misaligned expectations, miscommunications, or perhaps a need for better conflict resolution skills? Each of these revelations can guide them to specific areas for improvement. Furthermore, encourage them to set up small, manageable experiments in social settings to test new ways of interacting or coping with social pressure. This approach not only builds resilience but also improves their social skills through practical experience.

These skills help your teen not just bounce back from social setbacks but leap forward, equipped with deeper insights, refined skills, and a resilient mindset. This empowerment enables them to navigate their social world with confidence, viewing each challenge as a stepping stone to greater personal and social competence. As they continue to grow and face new challenges, the resilience they develop now will serve as a core strength, supporting their journey towards becoming well-rounded, emotionally intelligent adults.

### Celebrating Emotional Successes: Recognizing Growth

Recognizing and celebrating each forward step in the ongoing development of your teen's emotional intelligence is crucial in reinforcing their growth and motivation. Just as we track academic progress with grades and comments, marking emotional progress requires a systematic yet personal approach. Encouraging your teen to keep an emotional growth journal can be an effective way to do this. In this journal, they can record daily or weekly entries about situations that evoked strong emotions, their responses, and reflections on how they handled those feelings. Over time, this journal becomes a valuable tool for your teen to see their progress in handling complex emotions, increasing self-awareness, and improving their relationships. It's not just about recording events; it's about reflecting on them, which deepens their understanding and investment in their emotional journey.

The act of tracking these emotional milestones should be complemented by positive reinforcement, a powerful motivator that can transform the challenging path of emotional growth into an encouraging and rewarding experience. Celebrate these achievements, no matter how small they may seem. Did your teen handle a previously triggering situation with grace? Did they show remarkable empathy in a complex social interaction? Acknowledge these victories with sincerity and enthusiasm. You might set up a family dinner to celebrate these wins, or perhaps a special outing. What matters is that the celebration is tangible and meaningful to your teen, reinforcing their positive behaviors and encouraging them to continue developing their emotional skills.

Beyond the immediate family, the impact of role models who embody strong emotional intelligence can be profoundly inspiring for teenagers. Share stories of notable figures who have demonstrated exceptional emotional intelligence, such as Malala Yousafzai's empathy and resilience or Nelson Mandela's forgiveness and leadership. Discuss how these figures dealt with internal struggles, as well as what your teen could learn from their experiences. You can also highlight role models within your own community—teachers, family friends, or leaders who embody emotional intelligence. If possible, facilitate connections where your teen can learn directly from these role models, providing them with real-life examples of how emotional intelligence can be a powerful tool for personal and professional success.

Creating a family culture of emotional support is the foundation for nurturing your teen's emotional intelligence. This involves more than occasional discussions or scattered encouragement; it's about weaving emotional growth into the daily fabric of family life. Make it a habit to discuss emotions openly and without judgment, allowing each family member to express how they feel about various life situations. Encourage empathy by asking family members to consider each other's perspectives during these discussions. Additionally, foster an environment where emotional expressions, whether of joy, frustration, or sadness, are met with support and understanding rather than dismissal. This supportive atmosphere not only enhances each family member's emotional intelligence but also strengthens the emotional bonds within the family, creating a shared sense of understanding and respect that transcends the minutiae of daily interactions.

By integrating these practices into your daily life, you help create a nurturing environment that celebrates emotional growth, equipping your teen with the confidence and skills to continue their development. This ongoing recognition and support not only boost their self-esteem but also reinforce the importance of emotional intelligence in achieving a balanced and fulfilling life.

## Exercise: Emotion Exploration Workshop

### *Objective*

To enhance emotional awareness and expression through creative and interactive exercises.

### Materials

- Large sheets of paper or poster board
- Colored markers, crayons, or paint
- Emotion cards (with various emotion words written on them)
- Soft background music (optional)

### Instructions

1. Emotion Mapping (20 minutes):

- Give each participant a large sheet of paper and coloring materials.
- Ask them to draw an outline of a human body.
- Using the emotion cards as inspiration, have them color or draw where they feel different emotions in their body (e.g., anger might be red in the chest, joy could be yellow in the stomach).
- Discuss the completed emotion maps, comparing similarities and differences.

2. Emotion Charades (15 minutes):

- Take turns drawing emotion cards and acting out the emotion without words.
- Others guess the emotion being portrayed.
- After guessing, discuss how the emotion was expressed and recognized.

3. Emotional Storytelling (20 minutes):

- In pairs (teen and adult), create a short story incorporating at least three emotions from the emotion cards.
- Share the stories with the group, emphasizing how the emotions influenced the characters' actions and decisions.

4. Reflection and Discussion (15 minutes):

- Discuss what participants learned about emotions during the activities.
- Share any surprises or insights about how emotions are experienced and expressed.
- Talk about how understanding emotions can improve communication and relationships.

5. Emotion Action Plan (10 minutes):

- Each participant creates a personal action plan for practicing emotional awareness in the coming week.
- Share these plans and commit to checking in with each other about progress.

This activity workshop provides a fun, interactive way for teens and adults to explore emotions together, fostering deeper understanding and open communication about emotional experiences.

As we wrap up this chapter on emotional intelligence, your focus should center on the profound impact that recognizing, tracking, and celebrating emotional growth can have on your teen's development. These practices are not just about fostering emotional intelligence, but about creating a supportive environment that encourages continuous learning and emotional well-being. As we move forward, the focus will shift from internal growth to external expressions, exploring how these emotional skills manifest in personal relationships and social interactions, setting the stage for the next chapter on building effective and resilient personal connections. Remember, the journey of emotional intelligence is ongoing, and each step your teen takes is a victory worth acknowledging and celebrating.

## Sharing the Power of Building Social Skills

Earlier in this book, we explored the profound impact of the digital age on teen social interactions. We discussed how social media and online communication have become the new norm, reshaping how teens connect, express themselves, and build relationships. The digital landscape is just the tip of the iceberg. We've also explored the challenges of social anxiety, the importance of emotional intelligence, and the power of effective communication. These are all crucial components of social resilience, but so too is understanding how to navigate the complex digital social world our teens inhabit.

Building social skills in the digital age isn't about putting on a brave face behind a screen or hiding what we feel in cryptic posts. Quite the opposite. It's about learning to express emotions authentically online and offline, understanding that challenges in both realms are opportunities for growth, and developing the resilience to push through the inevitable awkward moments and missteps.

I hope that by this stage in your reading, you've seen how the strategies in this book can lead to positive choices such as encouraging open dialogue, setting healthy boundaries, and fostering independence while offering support. If the insights and activities in this book have made a difference in your approach to supporting your teen's social development, then you're in the perfect position to help other parents and teens.

**By leaving a review on Amazon, you'll help other readers discover the key steps they need to take to support their teens in developing crucial social skills in the digital age.**

Share your opinion of this book and a little bit about your own experiences applying its strategies. One of the most powerful ways to reinforce your own learning is to help others understand these important concepts.

**Please scan the QR code to leave a review.**

Thank you for your support. Together, we can shine a light on the transformative power of understanding and nurturing teen social skills in our rapidly changing world.

FIVE

# Building Confidence and Self-Esteem

A s parents, perhaps the most extraordinary gift you can offer your teens is the power of confidence—a robust sense of self-worth that transcends the fleeting approval of peers and the ephemeral highs of social media. This chapter delves into the bedrock of confidence, exploring how core beliefs about ourselves shape interactions and perceptions, both internally and externally. Self-esteem isn't just about feeling good; it's about recognizing and embracing one's capabilities and worth, even in the face of challenges and setbacks. This core strength enables teens to navigate life's complexities with resilience and grace.

### The Confidence Foundation: Building Self-Worth

The journey to solid self-esteem often begins with recognizing and celebrating one's accomplishments, no matter how small. As a parent, you play a crucial role in helping your teens discover and leverage their strengths. Encourage your teens to engage in activities that not only interest them but also challenge their abilities. Whether it's sports, the arts, coding, or volunteer work, active participation and gradual mastery provide tangible evidence of their capabilities, fostering pride. Each achievement builds upon their self-confidence, reinforcing their view of themselves as competent and capable individuals. It's important to acknowledge these achievements—not just the outcomes but also the effort and progress. This recognition anchors their self-worth beyond external validation, rooting their sense of self-value in something more substantial and enduring than transient external approval.

The internal narrative teens have about themselves shapes their self-image and, by extension, confidence. Positive affirmations are a powerful tool for reshaping this narrative. These are positive, first-person statements that are repeated regularly and reflect the qualities or goals teens aspire to. For instance, affirmations like "I am capable of achieving my goals," "I deserve respect from others and myself," or "I handle challenges with courage and grace" help to internalize these positive beliefs, countering the negative self-talk that can erode confidence. Encourage your teen to create a list of personal affirmations that resonate with their aspirations and challenges. Placing these affirmations in visible places—like mirrors, study areas, or journals—can serve as constant reminders of their inherent worth and strengths, silently reinforcing a positive self-image throughout the day.

Your role in nurturing your teen's self-esteem is paramount. Through your words, actions, and reactions, you can profoundly influence how your teen perceives and feels about themselves. It starts with demonstrating unconditional love and acceptance, conveying to your teen that they are valued primarily for being themselves, not just for their achievements or compliance. Rather than solely praising their successes, consistently express admiration for their effort and resilience. For example, commend them for working hard on a test, even if the grade wasn't perfect, or for standing up for a friend, highlighting the character shown rather than the outcome. Such encouragement helps teens internalize a sense of self-worth that's stable and independent of external accomplishments or others' opinions.

In today's digital age, teens are bombarded with curated glimpses into others' lives, often leading to unfavorable comparisons that can distort self-images and erode confidence. Discuss with your teen the skewed reality of social media, where individuals often showcase enhanced, filtered versions of their lives. Encourage them to be critical consumers of the content they consume, prompting them to question the reality behind the idealized images. Help them focus on their own journey and personal growth rather than comparing themselves to others. Activities like a "social media detox," where they take breaks from social media, can help reduce the impact of these comparisons by refocusing on offline activities that contribute to a sense of real accomplishment and joy. These discussions and activities help teens build a healthier self-image and value their own authentic experiences and achievements, reducing the insecurity that often comes from online comparisons.

## Exercise: Building a Confidence Vision Board

### Objective

To create a visual representation of your teen's strengths, goals, and positive self-image, reinforcing their self-esteem and confidence.

### Materials

- Large poster board or cork board
- Magazines, newspapers, or printed images

- Scissors
- Glue or pushpins
- Markers or colored pens
- Small notepad and pen for journaling

**Instructions**

1. Strength Identification (15 minutes):

- Have your teen write down 5-10 personal strengths or qualities they admire about themselves.
- Encourage them to think about compliments they've received or challenges they've overcome.

2. Goal Setting (15 minutes):

- Ask your teen to write down 3-5 social or personal goals they'd like to achieve.
- Ensure these goals are specific and achievable.

3. Positive Affirmations (10 minutes):

- Help your teen create 3-5 positive affirmations that resonate with them.
- Examples: "I am capable of making new friends," "I handle challenges with courage."

4. Image Collection (20 minutes):

- Have your teen look through magazines or online images to find pictures that represent their strengths, goals, and positive self-image.

- Encourage them to also find images of role models or inspirational quotes.

5. Vision Board Creation (30 minutes):

- Guide your teen in arranging and gluing the images, strengths, goals, and affirmations on the board.
- Encourage creativity in the layout and design.

6. Reflection and Sharing (15 minutes):

- Ask your teen to explain their vision board to you.
- Discuss how each element contributes to their confidence and self-esteem.

7. Display and Daily Reflection:

- Place the vision board where your teen can see it daily.
- Encourage a brief daily journaling session where they reflect on one element of their board and how it relates to their day.

8. Monthly Review:

- Schedule a monthly check-in to discuss the vision board.
- Update or add to the board as your teen grows and achieves goals.

You are laying a strong foundation of confidence that will support your teen through the challenges and triumphs of their formative years. This foundation not only enhances their current well-being but also equips them with the self-assurance to face the world with confidence and resilience, embracing opportunities to grow and thrive.

## Positive Self-Talk: Changing the Inner Dialogue

The conversations that occur within the quiet confines of our minds are just as critical as the ones we have with the world. For teenagers, these internal dialogues can often spiral into negative self-talk, undermining confidence and fostering self-doubt. You, as a parent, can play a pivotal role in helping your teen recognize and reshape these inner narratives into a source of strength and self-assurance.

The first step in this transformative process is helping your teen become aware of their self-talk. Negative or self-deprecating thoughts often operate just below the surface of consciousness, influencing emotions and behaviors without ever being fully recognized. These might manifest as beliefs like "I'm not good enough," "I can't do this," or "Everyone is better than me," which can erode self-esteem over time. Encourage your teen to tune into these thoughts, perhaps during moments of stress or frustration, and to capture them in writing. This act of identification is powerful; it externalizes thoughts and makes them easier to address.

Once these thoughts are recognized, the next step is to challenge and reframe them into more positive and empowering narratives. This process, often referred to as cognitive restructuring, involves questioning the validity of negative thoughts and replacing them with more constructive ones. For example, the thought "I always mess up" can be challenged with "Everyone makes mistakes; I can learn from this." Or, "I'm not good at this" can be reframed to "I'm not good at this yet, but I can improve with practice." These revised thoughts encourage a mindset of growth and possibility rather than one of limitation and defeat.

Encouraging your teen to practice this type of reframing can transform a moment of self-doubt into an opportunity for growth and self-compassion.

Keeping a self-talk journal can be incredibly helpful during this process. This journal should be a dedicated space where your teen can record negative thoughts that arise along with their more positive reframing. This not only helps in tracking patterns of negative thinking but also provides a tangible method for practicing and reinforcing positive self-talk. Over time, this journal can become a personal testament to your teen's ability to reshape their thinking, bolster their confidence, and provide a clear record of personal growth.

The overarching power of mindset in this journey cannot be overstated. The concept of a growth mindset posits that our fundamental qualities are things we can cultivate through our efforts. This belief is central to building genuine self-confidence, as it shifts the focus from achieving to improving oneself. As we reviewed in Chapter 4 when discussing resilience, understanding the difference between growth and fixed mindsets is crucial not only for resilience but also for developing increased self-esteem and confidence.

Unlike a fixed mindset, which views abilities and intelligence as static, a growth mindset thrives on challenge and sees failure not as evidence of unintelligence but as a springboard for growth and stretching our existing abilities. Fundamentally, this mindset changes how teens view challenges and setbacks, imbuing them with a sense of resilience and an understanding that abilities can be developed through dedication and hard work.

Explaining and modeling this mindset can have a profound impact on how your teen talks to themselves about their capabilities and challenges. It reinforces their belief that they are in control of their own abilities and that with effort, strategy, and input from others, they can grow and succeed.

By guiding your teen through these strategies—helping them recognize and reframe their inner dialogues, keeping a journal of their cognitive restructuring, and fostering a growth mindset—you empower them to cultivate a self-supportive and resilient inner narrative. These skills not only enhance their self-esteem but also equip them with the mental tools to face life's challenges from a place of strength and optimism.

### Overcoming the Fear of Rejection: Strategies for Resilience

Understanding the nuanced nature of rejection is crucial to helping your teen navigate their social landscape more confidently. Rejection, at its core, taps into some of our most primal fears—those of abandonment and isolation that trace back to our early ancestors, for whom exclusion from the group could have dire consequences. Today, while the stakes might not be survival, the emotional impact of rejection retains its potency. It's important to teach your teen that this fear isn't just normal; it's universal. Discussing the evolutionary roots of this fear can provide them with a broader perspective, helping them understand that their feelings of distress are part of a deeply ingrained human experience. This understanding can often be the first step in mitigating the sting of rejection, as it allows teens to feel less isolated in their experiences, fostering a sense of shared human vulnerability.

Rejection often feels deeply personal, like a direct assessment of one's essence or worth. As such, teaching teens to depersonalize rejection is essential to helping them develop resilience. It's crucial to convey that rejection can be caused by a multitude of factors that have nothing to do with their personal qualities or worth. For instance, a friend might decline an invitation not because they dislike the person inviting them, but because they have other commitments or are dealing with personal issues. Encourage your teen to consider these external factors, which often play a significant role in rejection. This shift in perspective can significantly alleviate the personal blame and shame that often accompany rejection. Framing rejection as a redirection rather than a personal failure can also be helpful. This viewpoint allows each rejection to be an opportunity to explore new avenues or relationships that might be more aligned with their values and interests.

Building emotional resilience against rejection requires more than just understanding and perspective; it necessitates active practice and skill development. One effective practice is the use of visualization techniques, where your teen can imagine facing a rejection scenario and handling it calmly and constructively. Guide them through envisioning the situation in detail—the setting, the people involved, what is said—and how they can respond in a way that maintains their self-esteem and dignity. Another powerful strategy is resilience training through exposure, which involves encouraging your teen to put themselves in low-risk social situations where rejection might occur, such as joining a new club or volunteering at a new organization. These controlled exposures can desensitize them to the fear of rejection and help them develop coping strategies in a safe environment.

Furthermore, establishing techniques like deep breathing, mindfulness, or focusing on physical sensations can help manage the immediate emotional turmoil that rejection can trigger. These techniques provide practical tools that your teen can use to regain their emotional balance in the face of rejection.

Encouraging reflection on past rejections is another valuable strategy for learning and growth. This reflection can be done through conversations or journaling, where your teen can explore what they learned from the experience, how they coped, and what they might do differently in the future. This process not only helps in processing the emotions associated with rejection but also transforms the experience from a purely negative event into a learning opportunity. Ask your teen questions like, "What did this experience teach you about your needs and boundaries?" or "How might you use this experience to strengthen your future interactions?" These reflections can foster a more proactive and empowered approach to social challenges, helping your teen view rejection as a normal part of life that holds valuable lessons and opportunities for self-improvement.

By incorporating these discussions, practices, and exercises into your parenting approach, you are providing your teen with tools not just to cope with rejection but to emerge from it stronger and more resilient. This skill set is invaluable, as it not only enhances their current well-being and social interactions but also lays the groundwork for handling the inevitable challenges of life with confidence and poise.

## Role Models and Mentors: Finding Inspiration

In the complex tapestry of adolescent development, the threads woven by role models and mentors hold a distinct place, providing guidance, inspiration, and practical examples of the kind of person a teen might aspire to become. Identifying and engaging with role models can significantly shape your teen's aspirations and behaviors, offering them tangible examples of success and the qualities needed to achieve it. Facilitating the identification of these figures is crucial for a parent. Encourage your teen to look for qualities that resonate with their own aspirations, whether in public figures, community leaders, teachers, or even within the family. This process involves more than just admiring someone's achievements;

it's about recognizing the qualities that helped them succeed, such as perseverance, integrity, empathy, and resilience.

Discussing the value of mentorship can have a profound impact on your teen's perspective on growth and development. Mentors provide more than just guidance; they offer support, wisdom, and a framework within which your teen can explore their identity and capabilities. A mentor acts as a sounding board and role model in real-time, offering both aspirational and practical insights. For instance, a coach or music teacher can guide your teen in developing specific skills as well as imparting life lessons like teamwork, discipline, and the importance of practice. Encourage your teen to actively seek out mentor relationships, whether through school programs, clubs, or community organizations. These relationships can provide them with a safe space to explore new ideas and challenges, bolstered by the support and guidance of someone they trust and respect.

Learning from the experiences of role models can also be incredibly inspiring. Encourage your teen to read biographies or watch documentaries about individuals they admire. This exploration can provide insight into the challenges these figures faced and how they overcame them. It's important for teens to understand that all successes come with trials and failures, and that resilience and persistence are often the keys to achieving one's goals. These stories can make the journey of their role models feel more relatable and attainable, reinforcing the idea that they, too, can achieve great things if they commit to their goals and learn from their setbacks.

Becoming a role model is an empowering goal for teens. It encourages them to embody the qualities they admire in others and act in ways that can positively influence those around them. Discuss with your teen how they can be a role model to younger siblings, peers, or community members. This could involve taking on leadership roles in school activities, volunteering for community service, or simply being a supportive friend. Encourage them to consider how their actions and choices can inspire others, emphasizing that they have the power to make a positive impact. This perspective can significantly enhance their self-esteem and sense of responsibility as they recognize the value and influence of their actions within their peer groups and communities.

By incorporating these elements—identifying role models, engaging with mentors, learning from others' experiences, and becoming a role model themselves—your teen is equipped not only to aspire to greater heights but also to lay a strong foundation for their personal and social development. This approach enhances their current adolescent experience and prepares them for future roles in society where they can continue to inspire and lead by example.

### Setting and Achieving Social Goals: Small Wins Matter

Setting achievable goals plays a crucial role in enhancing your teen's social skills and helping them become confident and socially competent individuals. This process starts with helping them set realistic social goals—targets that are specific, attainable, and tailored to their personal growth needs. This could include initiating conversations with peers, joining a club or group, or simply trying to spend more time with friends outside of school. The key here is to ensure that these goals are small enough to be comfortable, yet challenging enough to push their boundaries. For instance, if your teen is naturally introverted, a goal might be to initiate a conversation with one new person each week. This gradual approach helps build confidence without overwhelming them with too-high expectations. It's important to work closely with your teen to establish these goals and involve them actively in the process, so they feel ownership and responsibility for their social growth.

As these goals are set, the importance of recognizing and celebrating each achievement along the way cannot be overstated. Every small victory is a building block in the larger structure of self-confidence and social competence. Celebrate these milestones, whether it's your teen making a new friend, contributing to a group project, or attending a gathering they were initially anxious about. These celebrations can be simple acknowledgments or small rewards that recognize their effort and accomplishment. This practice not only reinforces positive behaviors but also motivates your teen, encouraging them to continue stepping out of their comfort zone. Maintaining an atmosphere of positivity and encouragement and focusing on their progress rather than perfection is key. This supportive environment is crucial in helping them persevere through social challenges and setbacks.

Introducing the concept of an accountability partner can further enhance your teen's commitment to their social goals. This partner could be a friend, a sibling, or even a parent—someone who checks in on their progress regularly, offers moral support, and keeps them motivated. This relationship adds a layer of accountability and support, making the goal-setting process more dynamic and interactive. For teenagers, knowing someone else is rooting for their success and aware of their objectives can be a powerful motivator. It also adds a social element to their goal achievements, making the process more enjoyable and less daunting. Encourage your teen to choose someone they trust and feel comfortable with as their accountability partner, and discuss how this partnership can help them move towards their social goals.

Flexibility in goal setting is another crucial aspect, as it allows for adjustments based on your teen's experiences and growth. As they progress, some goals may become too easy, while others might prove too ambitious. It's important to periodically review these goals with your teen, discussing what's working and what isn't. This review can be a regular part of the conversation with their accountability partner, where they can reflect on their progress and determine if any goals need to be adjusted. For example, if your teen has become comfortable initiating conversations with new people, they might shift their focus towards deepening existing relationships or participating in more public speaking opportunities. This flexibility keeps the goals relevant and challenging, but it also teaches your teen an important life skill: the ability to evaluate and adjust their strategies in various aspects of life based on ongoing results and changing circumstances.

Through these strategies—setting realistic goals, celebrating small victories, having accountability partners, and maintaining flexibility in their objectives—you are helping to scaffold your teen's social development in a structured yet adaptable way. This approach not only enhances their current social skills but also sets a pattern of continuous improvement and adaptation that they can apply throughout their lives in various settings beyond the social domain.

Exercise: Social Goal-Setting Workshop

### *Objective*

To create and implement a personalized social goal plan for both teen and parent.

### Materials

- Notebook or journal for each participant
- Pens or pencils
- Calendar or planner
- Stickers or small rewards for goal achievements

### Instructions

1. Goal Brainstorming (15 minutes):

- Both teen and parent individually write down 3-5 social goals they'd like to achieve.
- Goals should be specific, measurable, achievable, relevant, and time-bound (SMART).

2. Goal Sharing and Refinement (20 minutes):

- Discuss each other's goals.
- Help refine goals to ensure they're realistic and challenging.
- Select 1-2 primary goals for each person to focus on.

3. Action Plan Creation (20 minutes):

- For each primary goal, create a step-by-step action plan.

- Break down larger goals into smaller, weekly objectives.
- Identify potential obstacles and strategies to overcome them.

4. Accountability System (10 minutes):

- Decide on check-in frequency (e.g., weekly) and method (e.g., Sunday evening discussions).
- Create a simple tracking system in the notebook or planner.
- Agree on how to celebrate small victories (e.g., special treat, family movie night).

5. First Step Commitment (5 minutes):

- Each person commits to taking one small action toward their goal within the next 24 hours.
- Write down this commitment and share it aloud.

6. Ongoing Process:

- Hold regular check-ins as agreed.
- Adjust goals and strategies as needed.
- Celebrate achievements together.
- After a month, review overall progress and set new goals if needed.

This activity fosters a collaborative approach to social growth, allowing both parent and teen to work on personal goals while supporting each other. It demonstrates that social skill development is a lifelong process and helps strengthen the parent-teen relationship through shared goal-setting and achievement.

As we conclude this chapter on building confidence and self-esteem, remember the powerful role of goal-setting in shaping your teen's growth. Setting and achieving social goals provides tangible evidence of progress, reinforcing self-confidence and social competence. These small wins accumulate, creating a positive cycle of growth and achievement. Moving forward, the next chapter will explore navigating the social landscape, where these lessons in confidence and self-esteem will be put into practice, helping your teen interact with the world with assurance and grace.

SIX

# Navigating the Social Landscape

I magine that your teen stands at the edge of a maze. Each path represents a different social choice, each turn a potential shift in their journey of self-discovery. The walls of this maze aren't made of stone or hedge; they're constructed from the expectations, pressures, and influences of peers. Welcome to the social landscape of adolescence—a terrain as challenging as it is transformative.

As parents, we often wish we could hand our teens a map to navigate this complex world. But the truth is, there is no one-size-fits-all guide. Instead, what we can offer is a compass—a set of tools and strategies to help them find their way while staying true to themselves. This chapter is about equipping your teen with that compass, helping them understand the forces at play in their social world, and empowering them to make choices that align with their values and nurture their authentic selves.

Understanding Peer Pressure: Strategies to Stand Strong

Let's start a topic that affects almost all teens: peer pressure. It's a force as old as socializing itself, yet it takes on new dimensions in the teenage years. Peer pressure isn't always the dramatic, after-school special scenario we might imagine. More often, it's a subtle current, pushing and pulling our teens in ways they might not even recognize.

Defining peer pressure is the first step in understanding its impact. It's not just about being explicitly pressured to try drugs or skip class. Peer pressure is the influence that a group or individual has on someone to conform to certain behaviors, dress codes, or attitudes. It can be as subtle as the unspoken expectation to have the latest smartphone or as overt as being dared to break rules.

The tricky part? Peer pressure isn't inherently negative. It can push teens to strive for better grades, try out for sports teams, or volunteer in their communities. The key is helping our teens distinguish between positive influences that align with their values and negative pressures that push them away from their authentic selves.

Recognizing unhealthy influences is a crucial skill for teens to develop. Encourage your teen to tune into their inner voice—that gut feeling that something isn't quite right. Are they feeling anxious about fitting in? Do they find themselves acting in ways that don't align with their values? These are red flags that negative peer pressure might be at play.

Here's where the real work begins: equipping your teen with the tools to stand strong in the face of pressure. Assertiveness is like a muscle—it grows stronger with use. Start by role-playing scenarios at home. Practice phrases like, "I appreciate the invite, but I'm not comfortable with that," or "I understand that's your choice, but it's not for me." The goal isn't just to say no, but to do so with confidence and respect.

But standing strong isn't just about what you say—it's about who you surround yourself with. Encourage your teen to seek out friendships that uplift and support them. These are the friends who respect boundaries, celebrate differences, and make your teen feel valued for who they truly are.

Remember, navigating peer pressure is an ongoing process. Encourage your teen to reflect on their experiences through journaling. This practice not only helps process emotions but also serves as a roadmap for future encounters. By understanding their past responses to pressure, they can better prepare for future challenges.

### The Importance of Authenticity: Being True to Oneself

Now, let's talk about a concept that's at the heart of resilience and well-being: authenticity. In a world that often seems to demand conformity, being true to oneself is both a challenge and a superpower.

Exploring self-identity is a journey that lasts a lifetime, but it takes center stage during the teenage years. Encourage your teen to dive deep into self-discovery. This might look like keeping a personal journal, trying out different hobbies, or engaging in creative pursuits. The goal is to provide a safe space for your teen to explore who they are, free from judgment or expectation.

But here's the thing about authenticity—it requires courage. Being genuine, especially in group settings, can feel like standing naked in a crowd. It's vulnerable. It's risky. And it's absolutely necessary for building meaningful connections and a strong sense of self.

Talk to your teen about times when they felt pressured to mask their true selves. Maybe it was laughing at a joke they didn't find funny or pretending to like a movie everyone else loved. Now, contrast that with moments when they stood in their truth, even when it wasn't popular. How did each scenario make them feel? Often, we find that while authenticity might be uncomfortable in the moment, it leaves us feeling more aligned and at peace with ourselves in the long run.

Finding the balance between authenticity and conformity is a delicate dance. It's not about being obstinately different or refusing to adapt to social norms. Instead, it's about making conscious choices that honor your true self while still being respectful of others and the situation. Encourage your teen to think critically about their choices. Are they dressing a certain way because they genuinely like the style, or because they're afraid of standing out? Are they pursuing an activity because it excites them, or because it's what they think they "should" do?

Role-playing can be an incredibly effective tool for practicing authenticity. Set up scenarios where your teen might feel pressured to conform—maybe it's being invited to a party they're not comfortable attending, or being asked their opinion on a controversial topic. Practice responses that are true to their values while still being respectful of others. The goal isn't to create conflict, but to foster the confidence to stand in their truth. Let's try it out.

### Exercise: Authenticity Role-Play

#### *Objective*

To practice expressing authentic thoughts and feelings in challenging social situations while maintaining respect for others.

**Materials**

- Index cards
- Pen or pencil
- Timer (optional)

**Time:** 30-45 minutes

**Instructions**

1. Scenario Creation (10 minutes):

- Together with your teen, brainstorm 5-6 scenarios where they might feel pressured to conform or hide their true feelings. Write each scenario on an index card.
- Examples: a) Being invited to a party where you know alcohol will be served b) Friends pressuring you to skip class c) Being asked your opinion on a controversial political topic d) Feeling pressured to date someone you're not interested in e) Being encouraged to try a risky activity you're not comfortable with

2. Role-Play Preparation (5 minutes):

- Discuss the importance of balancing authenticity with respect for others.
- Remind your teen that the goal is to express their true feelings and values without creating unnecessary conflict.

3. Role-Play (15-20 minutes):

- Take turns drawing scenario cards.

- The parent plays the role of the person applying pressure, while the teen practices responding authentically.
- Spend about 3-5 minutes on each scenario.
- After each role-play, briefly discuss: • How did it feel to express your authentic thoughts? • What was challenging about the situation? • How did you balance being true to yourself with being respectful?

4. Reflection (5-10 minutes):

- Discuss overall takeaways from the exercise.
- Ask your teen: • Which scenarios felt most challenging? • Did you notice any patterns in how you responded? • How might you apply these skills in real-life situations?

5. Practice Phrases: Encourage your teen to develop a set of go-to phrases that feel authentic to them, such as:

- "I appreciate the invitation, but that's not really my scene."
- "I understand that's your view, but I see it differently."
- "I'm not comfortable with that, but I respect your choice."

Authenticity isn't about being perfect or having it all figured out. It's about being willing to show up as your imperfect, evolving self. Encourage your teen to embrace their quirks, their passions, and yes, even their flaws. These are the things that make them uniquely them.

## Making and Keeping Friends: The Value of True Connections

Friendships are the lifeblood of the teenage social world. They provide support, joy, and a sense of belonging. But not all friendships are created equal, and learning to cultivate meaningful connections is a skill that will serve your teen well into adulthood.

Let's start by exploring the qualities of lasting friendships. At their core, strong friendships are built on trust, respect, and mutual understanding. These are relationships where both parties feel seen, heard, and valued. Encourage your teen to reflect on their current friendships. Do they feel they can be themselves around their friends? Do they feel supported in their goals and respected in their choices? These are indicators of healthy, nurturing friendships.

Initiating and nurturing friendships can feel like a daunting task, especially for teens who might be naturally introverted or dealing with social anxiety. The key is to start small and focus on genuine connections rather than popularity. Encourage your teen to strike up conversations based on shared interests. Maybe it's complimenting a classmate's band t-shirt or asking about a book they're reading. These small interactions can be the seeds of deeper connections.

Role-playing can be incredibly helpful here too. Practice conversation starters and active listening skills. Remind your teen that showing genuine interest in others is one of the most attractive qualities a person can have. Encourage them to ask open-ended questions and really listen to the answers.

Of course, even the strongest friendships face challenges. Misunderstandings, jealousy, and conflicting priorities are all normal parts of relationships. The key is how we handle these bumps in the road. Teach your teen to approach conflicts with a mindset of curiosity rather than defensiveness. Instead of jumping to conclusions or assigning blame, encourage them to ask questions and seek to understand the other person's perspective.

Empathy and kindness are the glue that holds friendships together. These qualities create a safe space where both parties feel valued and understood. Encourage your teen to practice small acts of kindness—remembering a friend's important event, offering help without being asked, or simply being there to listen during tough times. These gestures might seem small, but they build a foundation of care and mutual support.

Remember, quality is more important than quantity when it comes to friendships. It's better to have a few deep, meaningful connections than a large circle of superficial acquaintances. Encourage your teen to invest time and energy into the relationships that truly nourish their soul and align with their values.

## Dealing with Bullying: Strategies for Teens and Parents

Bullying is a harsh reality that many teens face, and its impact can be devastating. As parents, it's crucial that we equip our teens with the tools to recognize, respond to, and recover from bullying situations. But let's be clear: bullying is not just "kids being kids" or a rite of passage. It's a serious issue that can have long-lasting effects on mental health, self-esteem, and overall well-being.

Recognizing bullying is the first step in addressing it. Bullying can take many forms—physical, verbal, social, or cyber. It's characterized by an imbalance of power, repetition, and intent to harm. Help your teen understand that bullying is never their fault and that they deserve to feel safe and respected.

It's important to note that bullying often happens in subtle ways. Social exclusion, spreading rumors, or even consistent "joking" that makes someone feel uncomfortable can all be forms of bullying. Teach your teen to trust their feelings—if something doesn't feel right, it probably isn't.

Empowering your teen with effective responses to bullying is crucial. This doesn't mean encouraging physical confrontation, but rather teaching assertiveness and self-advocacy. Role-play scenarios where your teen can practice using firm, clear language to stand up to a bully. Phrases like "Stop. I don't like that," or "That's not okay," delivered with confidence, can be powerful.

But let's be real—speaking up can be terrifying, especially when faced with a bully. That's why it's equally important to teach your teen about the power of allies. Encourage them to band together with friends or classmates who share their values. There's strength in numbers, and a united front can often deter bullying behavior.

Equally important is teaching your teen when and how to seek help. Emphasize that reporting bullying is not "tattling"—it's a brave and necessary step to ensure their safety and the safety of others. Help them identify trusted adults they can turn to, whether it's you, a teacher, a school counselor, or a coach.

As parents, our role in addressing bullying is multifaceted. We need to be vigilant for signs that our teen might be experiencing bullying—changes in behavior, reluctance to go to school, or unexplained injuries are all red flags. Create an open, non-judgmental space where your teen feels safe sharing their experiences.

This means being prepared to listen without immediately jumping into "fix-it" mode. Sometimes, our teens just need to be heard and validated. Ask questions like, "How did that make you feel?" and "What do you think you need in this situation?" This approach not only helps your teen process their experiences but also empowers them to be part of the solution.

If your teen is being bullied, take it seriously. Document the incidents, including dates, times, and any witnesses. Don't hesitate to advocate for your teen with school officials. Many schools have anti-bullying policies in place, and it's important that these are enforced. If you feel the school isn't taking appropriate action, don't be afraid to escalate the issue. Your teen's safety and well-being are paramount.

Building a support system is crucial for teens dealing with bullying. This network can include friends, family members, teachers, and mental health professionals if needed. A strong support system provides emotional comfort, practical assistance, and a sense of safety during challenging times.

Consider connecting your teen with a mentor—perhaps an older student or a trusted adult outside the family. Sometimes, teens find it easier to open up to someone who isn't a parent or teacher. This relationship can provide additional support and perspective.

Remember, recovering from bullying takes time. Be patient and continue to provide support even after the immediate situation is resolved. Encourage activities that boost your teen's self-esteem and help them reconnect with their strengths and passions. This might involve sports, arts, volunteering, or any activity where they can experience success and build positive relationships.

It's also important to address the possibility that your teen might be the one engaging in bullying behavior. This can be a difficult reality to face, but it's crucial to address it head-on. If you suspect your teen might be bullying others, approach the situation with empathy and a desire to understand. Often, teens who bully are dealing with their own insecurities or problems. This doesn't excuse the behavior, but understanding the root cause can help in addressing it effectively.

Lastly, let's talk about cyberbullying. In our digital age, bullying doesn't stop when school lets out. It can follow teens home via their devices, making it feel inescapable. Teach your teen about digital citizenship and online safety. This includes how to use privacy settings, the importance of thinking before posting, and how to report abusive behavior on social media platforms.

Encourage your teen to take screenshots of any bullying messages or posts as evidence. Many teens hesitate to report cyberbullying for fear of having their devices taken away. Assure your teen that seeking help won't result in punishment or loss of their digital privileges.

By addressing bullying comprehensively—recognizing it, responding to it, seeking help, and healing from it—we can create a safer, more supportive environment for our teens to thrive in.

## Social Media: The Good, The Bad, and The Ugly

In today's digital age, social media is an integral part of most teens' social landscapes. It's a tool that can connect, inspire, and inform— but it also comes with its own set of challenges and pitfalls. As parents, we need to help our teens navigate this digital world with wisdom and intentionality.

Navigating social media wisely starts with understanding its dual nature. On one hand, social media can be a platform for self-expression, creativity, and connection. It can help teens stay in touch with friends, explore interests, and even engage in social activism. Many teens find supportive communities online, particularly those who might feel isolated in their physical communities. For instance, LGBTQ+ teens in conservative areas might find acceptance and resources through online groups.

On the flip side, social media can also be a source of anxiety, comparison, and negativity. The curated nature of social media can create unrealistic expectations about body image, lifestyle, and success. It's crucial to have open conversations with your teen about the reality behind social media posts. Remind them that what they see is often a highlight reel, not the full picture of someone's life.

Discuss with your teen how to use social media intentionally. Encourage them to follow accounts that inspire and uplift them, rather than those that make them feel inadequate or negative about themselves. This might mean unfollowing or muting accounts that consistently make them feel bad about themselves, even if those accounts belong to friends or popular figures.

Talk about the importance of taking breaks from social media and engaging in real-world activities and face-to-face interactions. Many teens (and adults) find it helpful to set specific times for checking social media, rather than constantly scrolling throughout the day. Encourage your teen to try a "digital detox" for a day or a weekend and reflect on how it makes them feel.

Digital footprint awareness is crucial in this age of permanence. Help your teen understand that what they post online can have long-lasting implications. Encourage them to think critically before posting: Is this something they'd be comfortable with a future employer or college admissions officer seeing? Does it align with their values and the image they want to project?

This doesn't mean they can't be themselves online, but rather that they should be mindful of the potential consequences of their digital actions. Teach them about privacy settings and the importance of protecting personal information online.

Dealing with online negativity is unfortunately a common experience for many teens. Teach your teen strategies for handling cyberbullying, negative comments, and the pressure of comparison that often comes with social media use. This might include using blocking and reporting features, setting boundaries around social media use, and knowing when to step away from the digital world to protect their mental health.

Encourage your teen to be a positive force in their online communities. This could mean standing up against cyberbullying when they see it, sharing uplifting content, or using their platform to support causes they care about. Remind them that their online actions can have a real impact on others, for better or worse.

Discuss the concept of digital empathy—the ability to understand and share the feelings of others in online interactions. Encourage your teen to consider how their words might be interpreted without the context of tone and body language. Teach them to err on the side of kindness in their online communications.

It's also important to address the addictive nature of social media. Many platforms are designed to keep users engaged for as long as possible, which can interfere with sleep, homework, and real-life social interactions. Help your teen recognize signs that their social media use might be problematic, such as feeling anxious when they can't check their phone or losing track of time while scrolling.

Lastly, model healthy social media habits yourself. Be mindful of your own digital consumption and how you present yourself online. Your example can be a powerful influence on your teen's relationship with social media. This might mean putting your phone away during family dinners, avoiding mindless scrolling, and sharing your own reflections on how social media impacts your mood and behavior.

Remember, the goal isn't to demonize social media—it's a powerful tool that's here to stay. Instead, we want to empower our teens to use it wisely and intentionally, leveraging its benefits while mitigating its potential harms. By fostering open dialogue and critical thinking about social media, we can help our teens develop a healthy, balanced approach to their digital lives.

## Exercise: Social Scenario Role-Play Workshop

Now, let's put all of this into practice with an interactive workshop designed to help your teen navigate various social scenarios with confidence and authenticity.

### *Objective*

To practice navigating various social situations through role-play, enhancing communication skills and confidence.

### Materials

- Index cards with different social scenarios
- Timer
- Notepad for feedback

### Instructions

1. Together with your teen, brainstorm various social scenarios they might encounter. These could include dealing with peer pressure, resolving a misunderstanding with a friend, standing up to a bully, or navigating a difficult conversation on social media. Write each scenario on an index card.

2. Take turns drawing a card and acting out the scenario. The teen plays themselves, while the adult plays the other character(s). This gives your teen a chance to practice their responses in a safe, supportive environment.

3. After each 5-minute role-play, spend 5 minutes discussing:

- What went well?
- What could be improved?
- How did it feel to handle the situation?

4. Switch roles occasionally, allowing the teen to play different characters and the adult to model effective responses. This can provide your teen with new perspectives and strategies they might not have considered.

5. Conclude the session by discussing overall learnings and strategies that seemed most effective across different scenarios. What patterns emerged? What skills does your teen feel most confident about, and where do they feel they need more practice?

This activity provides a safe space for teens to practice social skills and receive constructive feedback, building their confidence for real-world interactions. It's also an opportunity for you to gain insight into the challenges your teen faces and how they approach problem-solving in social situations.

Navigating the social landscape of adolescence is no small feat. It requires courage, self-awareness, and a willingness to stand in one's truth even when it's uncomfortable. By guiding your teen through these aspects of social navigation—understanding peer pressure, embracing authenticity, cultivating meaningful friendships, addressing bullying, and navigating the digital world—you're equipping them with invaluable tools for not just surviving, but thriving in their social world.

Your role is to provide support, guidance, and a safe harbor as they learn to navigate these complex social waters. You're not just helping them develop social skills; you're nurturing their ability to form deep, meaningful connections while staying true to themselves. And in doing so, you're setting them up for a lifetime of rich, authentic relationships and a strong sense of self.

# SEVEN

# Activities for Building Social Skills

I n a period where the digital world frequently overshadows the physical, finding balance can feel like steering a boat through fog—challenging yet essential for reaching our destination safely. This chapter focuses on practical exercises that foster genuine connections, aiming to ground us in the tangible aspects of human interaction. These exercises are designed not just to draw us away from screens, but to bring us closer to one another, strengthening bonds through shared experiences that go beyond digital likes and comments.

As we begin this chapter, it's important to address a common concern: how do we convince teenagers to willingly participate in these family activities? Parents might already be anticipating resistance, while teens might be thinking these exercises sound unappealing or unnecessary.

The teenage years are typically a time of seeking independence, testing boundaries, and often, a desire to distance oneself from family activities. The suggestions in this book might initially seem unattractive to a teen. However, with the right approach, even skeptical teens can find value and enjoyment in these exercises.

## Understanding the Teen Perspective

It's crucial to recognize where teens are coming from. They're navigating a complex world of social pressures, academic stress, and personal identity formation. Their resistance often isn't about rejecting family, but about asserting their growing independence and individuality.

## Strategies for Engagement

1. **Involve Them in the Planning**: Instead of presenting activities as mandatory, include your teen in the decision-making process. Ask for their input on which activities interest them or how they might modify an exercise to make it more appealing.
2. **Explain the 'Why'**: Teens are more likely to participate if they understand the purpose. Have an open conversation about the goals of these activities – strengthening family bonds, reducing stress, improving communication – and how these skills can benefit them in their own lives.
3. **Start Small and Build**: Don't expect immediate enthusiasm for a full day of family activities. Begin with shorter, less intrusive exercises and gradually increase the time and complexity as comfort and interest grow.
4. **Make it Relevant**: Connect the activities to things your teen cares about. For example, if they're into sports, relate mindfulness exercises to improving athletic performance.
5. **Lead by Example**: Show your own willingness to try new

things. Share your experiences and the benefits you've noticed from these activities.

6. **Respect Their Space**: Recognize that teens need their alone time. Balance family activities with respect for their privacy and independence.

7. **Use Technology Positively**: Instead of framing these activities as anti-technology, find ways to incorporate tech positively. You might use a meditation app together or create a family playlist for background music during activities.

8. **Be Patient and Persistent**: Change takes time. Stay positive and keep offering opportunities for engagement without forcing participation.

The goal isn't to force teens into unwanted activities but to create an environment where they feel respected, heard, and genuinely interested in participating. With patience, understanding, and the right approach, even reluctant teens can come to appreciate and look forward to these family bonding experiences.

In the following sections, we'll explore specific activities designed to navigate the challenges of our digital age and reconnect with the physical world. We'll discuss how to tailor them to appeal to the teenage mindset, ensuring that your whole family, including your teens, can benefit from these exercises in connection and mindfulness. Our aim is to create a balanced approach that acknowledges the realities of our digital age while fostering the irreplaceable value of face-to-face human connections.

### Digital Detox Challenges: Promoting Offline Interaction

Imagine: it's Sunday morning, and instead of the usual symphony of notification pings and the glow of screens illuminating sleepy faces, there's... silence. Actual, honest-to-goodness silence. Welcome to the Digital Detox!

Without the constant digital noise, we suddenly have space. Space to talk, to laugh, to be bored together. We rediscover the art of eye contact and the joy of finishing a sentence without checking a notification.

This isn't about demonizing technology. It's about remembering that there's a whole world of joy and connection beyond our screens.

## Exercise: Plan a Digital Detox Day

Now, let's put this into practice with an interactive workshop designed to help your family disconnect from digital devices and reconnect with each other.

### *Objective*

To experience a full day without digital devices, promoting unfiltered, continuous real-world interactions and strengthening family bonds.

### Materials

- Calendar for planning
- List of offline activities
- Box or container for storing devices
- Journals or notepads for reflection

### Instructions

1. As a family, choose a day of the week to designate as your "digital detox day." Mark it on the calendar.

2. Create a list of offline activities that don't require digital devices. Include options for various interests and weather conditions.

3. On the chosen day, have each family member turn off their cell phones, tablets, and computers. Store them in a designated container.

4. Engage in the planned offline activities throughout the day. Encourage face-to-face conversations and collaborative activities.

5. At the end of the day, hold a family meeting to reflect on the experience. Discuss:

- What did each person enjoy most about the day?
- What challenges did they face?
- What did they learn about themselves and each other?

6. Plan how to incorporate more offline time into your regular daily life.

7. Schedule the next digital detox day, making it a recurring family event.

This activity creates a space where everyone can be fully present, engaging in conversation and reconnecting on a deeper level. It strengthens family bonds and fosters a healthier relationship with technology, reminding everyone of the joy that exists beyond the digital realm. However, it's important to recognize that this might be challenging at first, especially for those accustomed to constant digital connectivity. If that's the case, start small and gradually work your way up to a full day. Begin with a few hours of device-free time, then try a half-day, slowly increasing the duration as everyone becomes more comfortable with the practice. This gradual approach allows family members to adjust and discover the benefits at their own pace.

## Exercise: Creative Projects Without Screens

Imagine your family huddled around a giant canvas, paintbrushes flying. You're not just making art; you're building memories, sharing laughs, and having those rare, uninterrupted conversations. Maybe you'll write a story together, each adding your own twists. Suddenly, your 8-year-old's obsession with dinosaurs, your teenager's love for sci-fi, and your partner's terrible puns all come together in one hilariously bizarre tale.

These aren't just fun activities – they're stealth exercises for family bonding and brain power. You're nurturing creativity, critical thinking, and communication skills, all while creating inside jokes that'll last for years.

Let's explore how creativity can flourish in the absence of digital distractions.

### *Objective*

To engage in creative activities that promote self-expression, family bonding, and mental stimulation without the use of digital devices.

### Materials

- Art supplies (e.g., paints, brushes, paper, clay)
- Musical instruments (if available)
- Writing materials
- Any other craft supplies relevant to your chosen project

**Instructions**

1. As a family, brainstorm creative projects you'd like to try. Options might include:

- Painting or drawing
- Making music
- Writing stories or poems
- Crafting (e.g., knitting, woodworking, scrapbooking)

2. Choose one or more projects that interest everyone.

3. Gather the necessary supplies for your chosen project(s).

4. Set aside dedicated time for the family to work on the project(s) together.

5. As you create, encourage discussion about thoughts, feelings, and ideas inspired by the creative process.

6. Once the project(s) are complete, have each family member share their creation and what it means to them.

7. Reflect on the experience:

- How did it feel to create without digital assistance?
- What new things did you learn about yourself or your family members?
- How did this activity contribute to family bonding?

These exercises empower creative expression while also enhancing cognitive skills such as problem-solving and critical thinking. They develop familial ties through shared creative endeavors, celebrating both individuality and solidarity.

## Exercise: Outdoor Adventure Challenge

Want to see your kids' eyes light up with something other than screen glow? It's time to head outdoors!

Swapping Netflix for nature isn't just about escaping Wi-Fi range; it's about plugging into a whole new (or rather, very old) way of living. Whether you're hiking, biking, or just having a chaotic family game of tag, you're not just burning calories—you're building connections.

Picture this: Your family is tackling a local trail. Suddenly, your couch potato teen is leading the way, your usually shy 8-year-old is shouting encouragement, and you're all working together to decipher that suspiciously coffee-stained map. It's like a real-life video game, but with fresh air and no respawn button.

These adventures aren't just fun – they're secret weapons for family bonding. You're problem-solving, communicating, and high-fiving your way up that hill. Plus, you're all getting a healthy dose of vitamin D and exercise without a single complaint about "boring" workouts.

Best of all? You're showing your kids that the world is bigger than their screens. Now, let's venture outside and experience the freedom and connection that nature offers.

### Objective

To engage in outdoor activities that promote physical health, family cooperation, and appreciation for the natural world.

**Materials**

- Appropriate outdoor gear (depending on the chosen activity)
- Water and snacks
- First aid kit
- Map or trail guide (if necessary)

**Instructions**

1. As a family, choose an outdoor activity suitable for everyone's abilities. Options might include:

- Hiking a local trail
- Biking in a park
- Playing a team sport in the backyard
- Going on a nature scavenger hunt

2. Plan the details of your adventure, including location, duration, and any necessary preparations.

3. Assign roles to family members (e.g., navigator, photographer, snack coordinator).

4. During the activity, encourage cooperation and communication. For example:

- Navigate the trail together
- Cheer each other on during challenging parts
- Point out interesting natural features to one another

5. Take breaks to appreciate your surroundings and discuss what you're experiencing.

6. After the adventure, gather as a family to reflect:

- What was the most enjoyable part of the experience?
- What challenges did you overcome together?
- What did you learn about nature or each other?

7. Discuss how you can incorporate more outdoor activities into your regular routine.

These experiences are not only physically beneficial but also mentally and emotionally enriching. They provide fresh air, exercise, and the joy of achieving a goal together, while fostering an appreciation for nature and the environment.

### Exercise: Digital Detox Reflection Workshop

Digital detox complete, now for the fun part—the family debrief.

Huddle up and reflect. What worked well? What was tough? What surprises popped up when the screens went dark? This chat isn't just for warm fuzzies – it's cementing those screen-free lessons and plotting how to integrate more unplugged moments into daily life.

One day of digital detox is great, but a life peppered with screen-free adventures? That's the golden ticket. These little pockets of unplugged time are like seasoning in life's sometimes-bland casserole, reminding us that the world is a 3D experience no screen can match.

To conclude our digital detox challenges, let's reflect on our experiences and plan for the future.

*Objective*

To consolidate learnings from the digital detox experiences and integrate offline activities into daily life.

**Materials**

- Journals or notepads
- Pens or pencils
- Whiteboard or large paper for group brainstorming
- Calendar for future planning

**Instructions**

1. Gather as a family in a comfortable space.

2. Each family member should take a few minutes to write down their thoughts about the digital detox experiences, including:

- What they enjoyed most
- What they found challenging
- What they learned about themselves and others

3. Take turns sharing these reflections with the family.

4. As a group, discuss:

- How did the absence of digital devices affect family interactions?
- What unexpected benefits or challenges did you encounter?
- How did these experiences change your perspective on technology use?

5. Brainstorm ways to integrate more offline activities into your daily life. Write these ideas on the whiteboard or large paper.

6. Create a family action plan:

- Choose 2-3 offline activities to incorporate into your weekly routine
- Decide on the frequency of future digital detox days
- Assign responsibilities for planning and organizing these activities

7. Mark these plans on your family calendar.

8. Commit to reviewing and adjusting your plan monthly to ensure it continues to meet your family's needs.

This reflection process solidifies the lessons learned from these experiences, reinforcing the benefits of time spent offline. It provides a platform for discussing how to integrate more of these activities into regular daily life, ensuring that the digital detox isn't just a one-off event but part of a broader commitment to nurturing real connections and well-being.

## Emotional Intelligence Games: Learning Through Play

Integrating Emotional Intelligence (EI) games into your family's routine offers a wonderful method for enhancing your child's comprehension and management of emotions while fostering deeper family connections. These games, ranging from board games to role-playing situations, provide both fun and educational experiences that help develop essential emotional abilities such as empathy, acknowledgment, and guidance.

## Exercise: Empathy Board Game Night

Ever wish you could download empathy directly into your teen's brain? Well, we can't do that (yet), but we've got the next best thing: Empathy Board Game Night! It's time to dust off those board games and turn them into secret weapons of emotional intelligence. Imagine a family game night where the real prize isn't just winning, but understanding each other better. We're talking about games that'll have your teen considering others' feelings faster than they can say "You sank my battleship!" So, grab your dice, settle in, and get ready for a night of fun that sneakily builds emotional skills. Who knew Boardwalk could be a pathway to better relationships?

### *Objective*

To develop empathy and emotional understanding through interactive board games.

### Materials

- Empathy-focused board games (e.g., 'Empathy Is Your Superpower', 'The Compassion Game')
- Comfortable seating arrangement
- Snacks (optional, but recommended for a cozy atmosphere)

### Instructions

1. Choose an empathy-focused board game suitable for your family's age range.

2. Set up the game in a comfortable area where everyone can gather around easily.

3. Before starting, explain that the goal is not just to win, but to understand and relate to the emotions presented in the game.

4. As you play, encourage discussions about the emotions and situations presented in the game. Ask questions like:

- "How do you think this character feels?"
- "What would you do in this situation?"
- "Have you ever felt similar to this?"

5. After each round or significant moment in the game, take a brief pause to reflect on the emotional aspects of what just happened.

6. At the end of the game, have a family discussion:

- What new things did you learn about emotions?
- Did anyone surprise you with their insights?
- How can you apply what you learned to real-life situations?

7. Plan your next empathy game night, perhaps rotating game choices or allowing different family members to lead.

This exercise improves your teen's ability to relate well and opens up family conversations about feelings, making it easier to discuss sentiments and real-life circumstances.

### Exercise: Emotional Journey Video Game Session

Imagine using that game console for something other than virtual car theft or building block worlds. Welcome to the Emotional Journey Video Game Session, where button-mashing meets heartstring-tugging. We're talking about games that'll have your teen feeling all the feels—and then talking about them! It's like sneaking vegetables into a smoothie, but instead, we're blending emotional intelligence into gameplay. So, grab a controller, settle into the couch, and get ready to navigate digital worlds and real emotions together. Who knows? You might just level up your family's emotional intelligence while saving a virtual world or two.

### Objective

To use video games as a tool for exploring emotional situations and decision-making.

### Materials

- A video game console or computer
- Selected video games with emotional storylines (e.g., 'Journey', 'Rime')
- Comfortable seating for the family

### Instructions

1. Choose a video game known for its emotional storytelling or themes.

2. Before starting, explain that you'll be playing together to explore the emotional journey of the characters.

3. Take turns playing, or have one person play while others observe.

4. Pause the game at key emotional moments to discuss:

- What emotions is the character experiencing?
- What led to this emotional state?
- How is the character dealing with these emotions?
- What would you do in this situation?

5. After playing for a set time (e.g., 1 hour), have a family discussion:

- What was the most impactful emotional moment in the game?
- Did any character's emotional journey resonate with you personally?
- What strategies for handling emotions did you observe in the game?
- How can these insights apply to real-life situations?

6. Consider creating a family "emotional strategy guide" based on what you learned from the game.

By examining the emotional journeys within these games, you can assist your teen in pondering their own feelings and learn valuable lessons about emotional resilience and empathy.

### Communication Role-Play: Practicing Real-Life Scenarios

We're about to turn your living room into a bootcamp for budding conversationalists. Forget reading about communication skills—that's like trying to learn parkour from a PowerPoint presentation. Your teen needs to dive into the verbal obstacle course of real life, and role-playing is their safety harness. It's time to create a judgment-free zone where they can practice everything from negotiating curfew extensions to explaining suspicious dents in the car, all without the risk of actual grounding. Think of it as a live-action video game where leveling up means fewer foot-in-mouth moments and more "How did my kid get so articulate?" moments. So, grab your imaginary microphones and let the awkward begin —because in this game, embracing the cringe is how you win.

## Exercise: Difficult Conversations Simulator

Ever wish you could practice those cringe-worthy talks before they happen in real life? Well, now you can! Think of it as a flight simulator, but instead of learning to land a plane, you're learning to land points in a debate about curfew extension. We're creating a judgment-free zone where your teen can practice everything from confronting a gossipy friend to explaining a bad grade, all without the risk of actual consequence. It's like a real-life video game where the boss level is "Explaining to Dad why there's a dent in the car" without losing screen time privileges.

### *Objective*

To practice navigating challenging conversations and conflicts in a supportive environment.

### Materials

- Index cards with various difficult conversation scenarios
- Timer
- Optional: props to set the scene

### Instructions

1. As a family, brainstorm potential difficult conversations teens might face (e.g., confronting a friend about a betrayal, discussing a bad grade with a teacher).

2. Write each scenario on an index card.

3. Set up a "stage" area in your living room.

4. Take turns drawing a card and acting out the scenario. One person plays the teen, another plays the other party, and the rest of the family observes.

5. Act out the conversation for 5 minutes.

6. After each scenario, have a 5-minute family discussion:

- What strategies worked well?
- What could have been handled differently?
- How did it feel to be in each role?

7. Switch roles and try the scenario again, incorporating the feedback.

8. At the end of the session, reflect on:

- Common effective strategies across different scenarios
- Personal strengths and areas for improvement in communication
- How to apply these skills in real-life situations

This exercise helps teens develop a toolbox of responses, from de-escalating tension to asserting their viewpoint in a respectful way. It encourages them to consider the impact of their words and actions, fostering a deeper understanding of how to maintain relationships even through conflicts.

Exercise: Assertiveness Training Camp

It's time to help your teen find their voice without turning into a mini Gordon Ramsay. Think of it as charm school, but instead of teaching which fork to use, we're teaching how to use words to stand up for themselves. We'll practice scenarios ranging from

"No, I don't want to try that suspicious-looking substance" to "Actually, I disagree with that opinion." It's all about finding that sweet spot between doormat and jerk. So, lace up those metaphorical boots, and let's start training those assertiveness muscles.

### Objective

To practice assertive communication in various scenarios.

### Materials

- List of scenarios requiring assertiveness (e.g., setting boundaries, refusing peer pressure)
- "I statement" formula sheet: "I feel [emotion] when [situation] because [reason]. I would like [request]."
- Optional: video recording device for playback and analysis

### Instructions

1. Introduce the concept of assertiveness and its importance.

2. Review the "I statement" formula and practice creating a few as a family.

3. Present a scenario (e.g., "Your friend wants to copy your homework").

4. Have your teen respond assertively using the "I statement" formula.

5. Family members provide constructive feedback:

- Was the message clear?
- How was the tone and body language?
- Did it strike a balance between assertive and respectful?

6. If using a camera, review the recording together for additional insights.

7. Practice the scenario again, incorporating the feedback.

8. Repeat with different scenarios, rotating roles among family members.

9. Conclude with a reflection:

- Which scenarios were most challenging?
- How did it feel to communicate assertively?
- How can these skills be applied in daily life?

This training improves teens' interpersonal skills and boosts their confidence as they learn to stand up for themselves in various situations.

### Exercise: Interview Simulation Studio

Welcome to the Interview Simulation Studio, where we turn those nerve-wracking job interviews into Oscar-worthy performances. It's time to prepare your teen for the real world, one awkward handshake at a time. We're talking mock interviews that'll make your palms sweat but in a good way. From "Tell me about yourself" to "Where do you see yourself in five years?" (spoiler alert: not in this interview), we'll cover it all. We'll work on everything from firm handshakes to eye contact that says "hire me" instead of "help me."

*Objective*

To prepare teens for various interview situations through practice and feedback.

## Materials

- List of common interview questions
- Professional attire (optional, but can help set the mood)
- Video recording device (if possible)
- "Interview Feedback" sheets

## Instructions

1. Set up a mock interview space (e.g., a desk and two chairs).

2. Choose an interview scenario (job application, college admission, etc.).

3. Assign roles: interviewer, interviewee, and observers.

4. Conduct a 10-15 minute mock interview.

5. Observers take notes on:

- Verbal responses
- Non-verbal cues (eye contact, posture, gestures)
- Overall presentation

6. After the interview, provide constructive feedback:

- Interviewee shares how they felt
- Interviewer gives their impressions
- Observers share their notes

7. If recorded, watch the video together and discuss additional observations.

8. Practice specific elements that need improvement (e.g., answering a tricky question, maintaining eye contact).

9. Switch roles and repeat the process.

10. Conclude with a family discussion:

- What were the biggest learnings?
- How can these skills be applied to other life situations?
- Plan for ongoing interview practice sessions

This thorough approach ensures that teens not only learn how to express their thoughts clearly but also how to present themselves professionally, expanding their confidence and poise in real interview situations.

## Building a Support Network: Encouraging Peer Support

Navigating the teenage years can be like sailing through uncharted waters, where each social interaction can potentially either storm or sparkle. During this stage, the importance of a strong support network couldn't be greater. It provides a safety net to catch a teen when they falter, as well as a cheering squad to celebrate their triumphs.

## Exercise: Peer Support Group Starter Kit

It's time to help your kids find their tribe with our Peer Support Group Starter Kit. Think of it as building a real-life social network, minus the trolls and cat videos. We're creating a space where teens can share their dramas, traumas, and occasional "eureka!" moments with peers who get it. It's like a support group meets a cool hangout spot, where the only thing being shared is understanding (and maybe some snacks). Whether your teen is stressed about school, navigating the social jungle, or just trying to figure out why their left eyebrow won't cooperate, this group is their safe haven.

## Objective

To establish or join a peer support group that provides a safe space for teens to share experiences and solutions.

## Materials

- List of potential peer support group themes
- Guidelines for respectful communication
- Notebook for planning meetings
- Snacks (because teens + food = success)

## Instructions

1. Discuss with your teen the concept of a peer support group and its benefits.

2. Brainstorm potential themes for the group (e.g., academic stress, social dynamics, personal growth).

3. Decide whether to join an existing group or start a new one:

- If joining: Research local groups and attend a meeting together
- If starting: Move to step 4

4. For a new group:

- Help your teen invite peers who might be interested
- Choose a regular meeting time and place
- Establish group guidelines for respect and confidentiality

5. Plan the first meeting:

- Create an icebreaker activity
- Prepare a topic for discussion
- Set up the meeting space to be welcoming and comfortable

6. After the first meeting, reflect with your teen:

- What went well?
- What could be improved?
- How did it feel to share and listen to peers?

7. Encourage regular attendance and possibly rotating leadership roles.

8. Check in periodically about the group's impact and any support needed.

The beauty of these groups lies in their foundation of mutual respect and empathy, which can significantly enhance each member's ability to cope with stress and build resilience.

### Exercise: Mentorship Match-Up

We're on a mission to connect your budding teenager with a wise sage who's been there, done that, and got the t-shirt (probably with an inspirational quote on it). This isn't about finding someone to nag them about homework; it's about discovering a guide who can show them the ropes of life, career, or maybe just how to adult without burning down the kitchen. Whether your teen is a budding artist, a future CEO, or just trying to figure out their path, we'll help them find a mentor who can light the way.

*Objective*

To connect teens with mentors who can provide guidance, encouragement, and support.

## Materials

- List of your teen's interests and goals
- Directory of local mentorship programs
- Notebook for mentor meeting notes

## Instructions

1. Sit down with your teen and discuss the concept of mentorship:

- What is a mentor?
- How can a mentor be helpful?
- What qualities would they want in a mentor?

2. Make a list of your teen's interests, goals, and areas where they'd like guidance.

3. Research mentorship opportunities:

- School programs
- Community organizations
- Professional associations in areas of interest

4. Help your teen reach out to potential mentors or mentorship programs.

5. Prepare for the first mentor meeting:

- Brainstorm questions to ask
- Set some initial goals for the mentorship

6. After the first meeting, reflect with your teen:

- How did it go?
- Do they feel this mentor is a good fit?
- What do they hope to gain from the relationship?

7. Encourage regular check-ins about the mentorship:

- What are they learning?
- How is it helping them grow?
- Are there any challenges?

8. If your teen shows leadership potential, discuss the possibility of them becoming a mentor to younger peers.

Mentors can help teens set realistic goals, encourage them to step out of their comfort zones, and provide a safe space to discuss fears and disappointments without judgment.

## Exercise: Community Service Adventure

Welcome to the Community Service Adventure, where we're saving the world one good deed at a time. It's like a family vacation, but instead of getting sunburned and arguing over maps, you're making a difference and feeling warm fuzzies. We're talking about activities that'll have your teen realizing that "influencer" can mean more than just having a million followers. From serving meals at a soup kitchen to planting trees or teaching grandma how to video call, we're about to embark on a journey that's part charity, part family bonding, and all heart.

*Objective*

To engage in community service activities that build connections, instill a sense of purpose, and develop social empathy.

## Materials

- List of local volunteer opportunities
- Calendar for planning
- Any necessary supplies for the chosen activity

## Instructions

1. As a family, research local community service opportunities:

- Local clean-up events
- Food banks
- Animal shelters
- Senior centers or healthcare centers
- Environmental conservation projects

2. Discuss which causes resonate most with your family values.

3. Choose a community service activity that everyone can participate in.

4. Prepare for the activity:

- Sign up or register if necessary
- Gather any required supplies
- Discuss expectations and goals

5. Participate in the chosen community service activity together.

6. After the activity, have a family reflection session:

- What did each person enjoy most?
- What was challenging?
- What did you learn about the community or each other?
- How did it feel to make a difference?

7. Discuss how to make community service a regular part of your family routine.

8. Plan your next service activity, perhaps trying something new or building on this experience.

These activities can significantly widen a teen's circle of connections and develop their understanding of teamwork and community engagement. Moreover, working toward a shared goal can create a sense of camaraderie and accomplishment among participants, strengthening the bonds between them.

### Family Activities: Strengthening Bonds and Skills Together

Family time is more than just an opportunity to be together; it's a chance to weave stronger social threads that not only connect but also fortify each family member against life's inevitable challenges. Organizing activities that involve all family members can transform everyday moments into memories and lessons that last a lifetime.

### Exercise: Family Game Night Championship

Forget about mind-numbing screen time; we're talking old-school, face-to-face fun that'll have everyone forgetting to check their phones. From classic board games to charades that'll leave you in stitches, we're creating a weekly tradition that's part bonding, part brain-teasing, and all awesome. It's a chance for your teen to showcase their strategic brilliance, for Dad to finally use that obscure trivia knowledge, and for Mom to reveal her hidden talent for miming "underwater basket weaving." Let's turn game night into the highlight of the week!

### Objective

To foster communication, cooperation, and healthy competition through regular family game nights.

### Materials

- A variety of board games, card games, or interactive games
- Scoreboard or trophy (optional, for added excitement)
- Snacks and beverages
- Calendar for scheduling

### Instructions

1. As a family, choose a regular night for your game championship (e.g., every Friday).

2. Create a roster of games that appeal to different family members, including:

- Strategy games
- Cooperative games
- Quick, fun games
- Educational games

3. Establish some ground rules for fair play and good sportsmanship.

4. On game night:

- Take turns choosing the game
- Mix up teams or partnerships if applicable
- Encourage discussion and laughter throughout

5. After each game, have a quick debrief:

- What strategies worked well?
- How did teamwork play a role?
- What was the most enjoyable part?

6. Keep a running scoreboard or pass a trophy to create a sense of ongoing championship (if desired).

7. At the end of each month, reflect as a family:

- What were the favorite games?
- How has game night affected the family dynamic?
- Any new games to add to the rotation?

These game nights' laughter and camaraderie can significantly strengthen familial bonds, making them cherished traditions that reinforce the family as a unit.

### Exercise: Master Chef Family Edition

Attention all kitchen novices and culinary maestros! It's time to turn dinner prep into a delicious adventure with Master Chef Family Edition. We're not just cooking meals; we're serving up a big plate of family bonding with a side of life skills. Picture this: your teen chopping veggies (with all fingers intact), your partner mastering the art of not burning water, and you orchestrating it all like a seasoned conductor. It's part cooking show, part comedy routine, and all delicious. We'll tackle family recipes, explore new cuisines, and maybe even invent a dish or two (Spaghetti Tacos, anyone?). Along the way, we'll stir in some teamwork, sprinkle in some problem-solving, and garnish it all with hearty laughs. Let's turn dinner prep into a delicious adventure!

### *Objective*

To transform meal preparation into a collaborative family activity that teaches life skills, encourages teamwork, and creates opportunities for meaningful conversations.

### Materials

- Recipes (family favorites or new challenges)
- Cooking utensils and ingredients
- Aprons for everyone (optional, but fun!)
- Music playlist for cooking ambiance

### Instructions

1. Choose a regular day for family cooking (e.g., Sunday dinners).

2. As a family, plan the menu:

- Rotate who gets to choose the main dish
- Ensure everyone has a role in the meal preparation

3. Assign roles based on age and ability:

- Younger kids can measure or mix
- Teens can take on more complex tasks
- Adults can supervise and handle any dangerous tasks

4. Before cooking, have a quick "team meeting":

- Review the recipe and game plan
- Discuss any potential challenges
- Assign a timekeeper to keep things on schedule

5. Cook together, encouraging conversation throughout:

- Share family stories or traditions related to the dish
- Discuss everyone's day or upcoming events
- Ask open-ended questions to spark deeper discussions

6. Set the table together and enjoy the meal as a family.

7. During the meal, reflect on the cooking process:

- What was the most enjoyable part?
- What new skills did everyone learn?
- How did teamwork contribute to the final result?

8. Plan the next family cooking session, perhaps with a new cuisine or cooking challenge.

This activity not only teaches valuable life skills like cooking but also fosters coordination and communication in a relaxed setting. The conversations that flow while chopping vegetables or stirring a pot often delve into topics that might not arise in more formal settings, creating a casual atmosphere where family members are comfortable opening up about various subjects.

### Exercise: Cultural Exploration Expedition

Pack your imaginary bags and grab your metaphorical passports – it's time for a Cultural Exploration Expedition, right from your living room! We're turning your home into a launchpad for world-wide adventures, no jet lag required. Each month, we'll "visit" a new country or culture, immersing ourselves in everything from its cuisine to its customs. It's like a crash course in global citizenship, but with comfier seating. We'll learn to say "hello" in new languages, attempt to recreate iconic dishes (with varying degrees of success), and maybe even try on traditional outfits (embarrassing family photos, anyone?). It's a chance to broaden horizons, challenge stereotypes, and maybe discover that your teen has a hidden talent for Bollywood dancing or origami. So, spin that globe, pick a destination, and let's embark on a journey that'll make your family the most cultured on the block.

### Objective

To broaden family perspectives and foster curiosity about different cultures through planned cultural exploration activities.

### Materials

- World map or globe
- Cultural exploration resources (books, documentaries, websites)
- Materials for related crafts or activities
- Ingredients for cooking cultural dishes (if applicable)

### Instructions

1. As a family, choose a culture or country to explore each month.

2. Create a "Cultural Exploration Checklist" for each expedition:

- Learn basic phrases in the language
- Cook a traditional meal

- Watch a film or documentary about the culture
- Create art inspired by the culture
- Listen to traditional music
- Read a book by an author from that culture

3. Designate roles for each family member in the exploration:

- Cultural Cuisine Chef
- Language Learner
- Art Director
- History Buff
- Music Maestro

4. Throughout the month, engage in activities from your checklist.

5. Have a "Cultural Celebration Night" at the end of the month:

- Prepare and enjoy a meal from the culture
- Share what each person learned in their role
- Discuss similarities and differences with your own culture
- Reflect on how this exploration changed your perspectives

6. Choose the next culture to explore, perhaps letting a different family member pick each time.

These cultural exploration activities can significantly expand your family's perspectives, fostering a sense of curiosity and openness. They provide a context for discussing different viewpoints and narratives, enhancing your teens' understanding of the world. Such experiences can spark interest in areas your teen may not have encountered otherwise, potentially leading to new hobbies or academic interests.

As we wrap up this chapter, let's take a moment to appreciate the power of these family activities. They're more than just ways to pass the time; they're opportunities to strengthen your family bonds and help your teens develop crucial life skills.

Each exercise, from game nights to volunteer projects, serves a dual purpose. They're fun in the moment, sure, but they're also building blocks for your teen's future. We're talking about developing empathy, honing communication skills, and fostering a sense of community responsibility - all disguised as family time.

These shared experiences create a tapestry of memories and learning moments. They transform ordinary days into opportunities for growth, extending your family's connections both with each other and the wider world. They help cultivate compassion, teamwork, and social awareness in ways that lectures or rules simply can't match.

As you move forward, remember that these activities aren't just about today. They're shaping your family's story and equipping your teens with valuable skills and perspectives they'll carry into adulthood. The conversations you have, the challenges you overcome together, and the memories you create - these are the threads that will continue to connect your family, even as your teens grow and change.

So, keep at it, parents. These shared moments aren't just shaping your days; they're molding your family's future, creating bonds and developing abilities that will resonate far beyond the time spent together. Your investment in these activities is an investment in your family's long-term happiness and your teen's future success.

# EIGHT

# Supporting Your Teen's Journey

Navigating the teenage years can often feel like deciphering a complex map without a legend, especially when it comes to communication. Every interaction, every silence, holds a nuance that can seem puzzling at first. However, as you embark on guiding your teenager through these formative years, the power of open and effective communication cannot be overstated. It forms the foundation upon which trust is built and understanding grows, enabling your teen to confidently explore their social, emotional, and academic landscapes.

## Starting the Conversation: Tips for Open Dialogue

Creating a safe space for dialogue is crucial. Teens need to feel that their thoughts and feelings are respected and valued. This goes beyond just providing a quiet, comfortable physical setting; it's about cultivating an emotional atmosphere where they feel secure. Start by affirming your teen's perspective, showing appreciation for their openness, and validating their feelings, even when you don't fully understand or agree with them. This doesn't mean refraining from guidance or feedback, but rather ensuring that your initial response is one of acceptance. Such an environment encourages your teen to share more freely and honestly, reducing the fear of judgment or dismissal.

Active listening is a skill that requires practice and patience, especially with teenagers whose communication styles can be as varied as their moods. To master this art, focus on truly hearing what your teen is saying without planning your response or judgment. This involves giving them your full attention—putting aside devices, making eye contact, nodding, or making small verbal acknowledgments to show you're engaged. Consider what you've heard by summarizing their points, asking clarifying questions, and expressing empathy. For instance, if your teen is upset about falling out with a friend, you might say, "It sounds like you're really hurt because you feel betrayed. Is that right?" Such responses demonstrate that you're listening and connecting with their emotional experience.

Keeping the conversation flowing often relies on how questions are framed. Open-ended questions, as opposed to those with yes or no answers, encourage deeper reflection and more elaborate responses, paving the way for richer dialogue. Instead of asking, "Did you have a good day at school?" try, "What was the most interesting thing you learned today?" or "How did the group project discussion go?" These questions invite your teen to share their thoughts and feelings in more depth, providing insights into their world and helping you understand their perspectives better.

Regular check-ins are vital for maintaining open lines of communication. Sometimes, the rhythm of our daily lives can sweep us along, making it easy to let communication with our teen become transactional—about schedules, chores, and responsibilities. Instituting regular, casual check-ins can break this pattern, ensuring ongoing open dialogue. These check-ins can be as simple as a chat over a snack after school or a walk after dinner. Consistency and a non-pressuring atmosphere are key. These moments signal to your teen that their life and feelings are important to you, regardless of the busyness of life. They provide a regular touchpoint that can help you catch early signs of issues or changes in your teen's mood or behavior, as well as offer timely support or intervention.

### Exercise: Communication Role-Play

Get ready to step into each other's shoes and flex those communication muscles! We're turning your living room into a stage for the great parent-teen dialogue. It's like improv comedy, but with less laughs and more "I statements." We'll tackle scenarios ranging from the dreaded "bad grade discussion" to the classic "but all my friends have a later curfew" debate. You'll get to experience life on both sides of the parental divide, potentially discovering that being a teen isn't all TikTok dances and memes, and being a parent isn't just about saying "because I said so." It's a chance to practice open-ended questions, active listening, and creating a judgment-free zone, all while potentially uncovering your hidden talent for diplomatic negotiations. So, clear your throat, put on your best active listening face, and let's dive into some role-play that might just revolutionize your family's communication game.

### *Objective*

To improve family communication skills and build empathy through role-playing exercises.

**Materials**

- List of scenario ideas
- Timer (optional)
- Notepad for observations (optional)

**Instructions**

1. Choose a scenario from the list or create your own. Some ideas include:

- Discussing a poor grade
- Negotiating a later curfew
- Addressing a disagreement with a friend
- Talking about college or career plans
- Discussing social media usage

2. Decide who will play the parent and who will play the teen for the first round.

3. Set the scene and begin the role-play. Try to stay in character for 5-10 minutes.

4. During the role-play, focus on:

- Using open-ended questions
- Practicing active listening
- Creating a safe, non-judgmental space for dialogue
- Expressing emotions clearly and respectfully

5. After the role-play, take a few minutes to discuss:

- What felt comfortable or uncomfortable?
- What techniques worked well?

- What would you do differently next time?
- How did it feel to be in the other person's position?

6. Switch roles and choose a new scenario for another round.

7. After a few rounds, reflect as a family:

- What did you learn about each other's perspectives?
- How can you apply these skills in real-life conversations?
- What areas of communication do you want to improve as a family?

This exercise can help both parents and teens develop better communication skills, build empathy for each other's perspectives, and create a foundation for more open and effective dialogues in the future. Plus, you might discover your family has a knack for improvisational theater – future family talent show, anyone?

### Setting Healthy Boundaries: Online and Offline

In a digital landscape that evolves at an ever-rapid pace, guiding your teen to navigate their online and offline lives safely and responsibly requires a delicate balance. It's about setting limits and protection while also fostering a sense of moral responsibility and independence.

Discussing internet safety is as much about protecting your teen from external threats as it is about educating them on the responsibilities that come with digital freedoms. Initiating open discussions about the risks of online activity lays the groundwork for a safer digital environment. It's crucial to discuss common pitfalls such as oversharing personal information, engaging with strangers, and encountering inappropriate content. Providing clear, age-appropriate guidelines helps teens understand what safe online behavior looks like. For example, discussing the implications of sharing personal details and the permanence of online posts can encourage more thoughtful interactions with digital content.

Balancing the freedom teens crave with the oversight necessary for their safety is challenging but crucial. As teens push for more independence, it's important to gradually expand their freedoms while maintaining a safety net. To strike this balance, establish boundaries that gradually broaden as your teen demonstrates maturity and understanding of safe practices. For instance, you might start with strict limits on social media time, which could be relaxed as your teen shows they can handle the responsibility without it affecting their other obligations or emotional well-being.

The issue of privacy versus monitoring is particularly thorny for many families. While it's important to respect your teen's need for private conversations and space, both online and offline, it's equally important to ensure their activities are safe and appropriate. Finding a balance often comes down to open communication about the level of monitoring you believe is necessary, why it's needed, and how it will be conducted. Rather than covert surveillance, opt for a transparent approach where your teen is aware of the monitoring and the reasons for it. This could mean having access to their social media accounts but respecting their space by not commenting on every post or conversation they're part of unless there's a safety concern. This transparency helps build trust and understanding, demonstrating that your primary concern is their safety rather than controlling their social interactions.

Negotiating rules together can be one of the most effective ways to ensure that boundaries are respected. When teens are involved in drawing their own lines, they're more likely to adhere to them. This process should be collaborative, allowing both parents and teens an opportunity to express their concerns and preferences. For example, you and your teen could work together to create a 'digital curfew' — a time at night after which all devices are put away. Additionally, discussing and setting rules about meeting online friends in person can be crucial for safety. These conversations should emphasize mutual respect for each other's viewpoints and a shared commitment to safety.

## Encouraging Independence While Offering Support

Fostering decision-making skills is essential because it directly impacts their ability to handle challenges, opportunities, and make the day-to-day choices that shape their lives. Facilitate this growth by involving your teen in everyday decisions that affect them, from choosing weekly meal plans to deciding which extracurricular activities to join. This inclusion not only makes them feel valued but also enhances their ability to weigh options and anticipate outcomes.

When discussing bigger decisions, such as high school courses or summer jobs, guide them through a structured decision-making process. This can involve identifying goals, gathering information, considering potential outcomes, and evaluating alternatives. For example, if your teen is deciding which subjects to choose, discuss their long-term goals, research the subjects' requirements and implications for future college applications, and consider their interests and aptitude in each subject. Encourage them to list pros and cons, and allow them the space to make the final decision. It's also important to discuss the benefits of making choices that don't turn out as planned. Emphasize that each decision is a learning opportunity, opening up the possibility that 'mistakes' are often just steps toward greater wisdom.

Supporting without solving is a delicate balance. As your teen inevitably faces challenges they need to learn to handle independently, your instinct to protect and solve problems can be strong. Resisting this urge and instead supporting them in finding their own solutions is key to fostering their problem-solving skills and resilience. Start by being a good listener when your teen shares a problem, fighting the temptation to offer solutions immediately. Instead, ask guiding questions that encourage them to think critically and explore potential options. For instance, if they're dealing with a conflict with a friend, rather than suggesting what they should do, ask, "What do you think might help resolve this situation?" or "What outcome are you hoping for from this conflict?"

Encouraging exploration of interests is vital during the teenage years. One of the joys of adolescence is the discovery of new passions that can influence career choices and lifelong hobbies. Encourage your teen to explore various interests by providing opportunities to try new activities. This could mean enrolling them in diverse classes, from art to coding, or encouraging participation in various clubs and sports. Maintain an open dialogue about what they enjoy or dislike about each activity, helping them to reflect on and understand their preferences.

Teaching financial independence is a critical life skill that promotes independence and responsibility. Begin by discussing budgeting basics. Help them create their own budget, perhaps starting with managing their allowance or earnings from part-time work. Teach them to track their income and expenses, set saving goals, and make informed spending decisions. Budgeting apps and spreadsheets can make this process more engaging and tangible. Involve your teen in age-appropriate family financial discussions. Explain the reasoning behind how you budget for family expenses, savings, and investments, as well as the financial considerations for family decisions like vacations or major purchases. This openness demystifies financial management and prepares them for their financial responsibilities in adulthood.

## Exercise: Personal Interest Project

Whether your teen has always dreamed of writing the next great American novel, coding an app that'll make Mark Zuckerberg jealous, or starting a dog-walking empire, now's their time to shine. Think of it as their own personal Shark Tank, minus the intimidating billionaires and with 100% more supportive parents. Grab your thinking caps, dust off those ideas you've been hiding, and let's turn your family's passion into a project that you'll all be excited about

### *Objective*

To encourage independence, foster creativity, and develop project management skills through the planning and execution of a personal interest project.

### **Materials**

- Notebook or digital document for project planning
- Calendar for timeline creation
- Resources related to the chosen project (books, online tutorials, supplies, etc.)
- Vision board materials (optional)

**Instructions**

1. Brainstorm and Choose:

- Have your teen list their interests, hobbies, and dream projects
- Discuss the feasibility of each idea
- Choose one project to focus on (e.g., creating a short film, learning a new language, starting a small business)

2. Set Goals and Create a Timeline:

- Help your teen define clear, achievable goals for their project
- Break the project into smaller, manageable tasks
- Create a timeline for completing each task
- Consider using a visual aid like a Gantt chart or a simple calendar

3. Plan and Gather Resources:

- Encourage your teen to research what they'll need for the project
- Help them identify and acquire necessary resources
- Discuss potential challenges and brainstorm solutions

4. Execute and Monitor:

- Let your teen take the lead in project execution
- Schedule regular check-ins (weekly or bi-weekly) to discuss progress
- During check-ins, ask open-ended questions like:

- What's been the most exciting part so far?
- What challenges have you faced, and how did you over-come them?
- What's your next step?

5. Provide Support:

- Offer guidance when asked, but resist the urge to take over
- Help your teen problem-solve when they hit roadblocks
- Provide encouragement and acknowledge their efforts

6. Reflect and Celebrate:

- Upon completion, have a "Project Showcase" where your teen presents their work
- Discuss what they learned about the subject and about themselves
- Celebrate their effort, creativity, and perseverance, regardless of the outcome
- Consider how this project might influence future goals or interests

Remember, the goal isn't perfection – it's growth, learning, and building confidence. This project is a chance for your teen to explore their interests, develop valuable skills, and maybe even discover a lifelong passion. Who knows? This could be the start of the next big thing, or at least a really cool story for future job interviews!

### Celebrating Progress: Acknowledging Efforts and Achievements

Celebrating progress and acknowledging efforts and achievements is crucial in the intricate dance of raising teens. It's about recognizing the small victories and incremental advancements that often go unnoticed in the daily hustle. Celebrating these moments can significantly impact your teen's motivation and self-esteem, turning even the smallest triumphs into springboards for future accomplishments. As parents, fostering an environment where every effort is acknowledged not only builds a supportive atmosphere but also instills a sense of accomplishment and pride in your teenager.

Recognizing small victories is essential because it reinforces the positive behaviors and efforts that lead to these achievements. For instance, if your teen has been struggling with math and their grade improves even slightly, it's a moment worth celebrating. This doesn't require grand gestures; sometimes, acknowledgment can be as simple as a congratulatory note on the refrigerator or a special mention at dinner. These affirmations make the effort tangible, showing your teen that their hard work isn't going unnoticed. It's about validating their journey and making the connection between perseverance and results clear and rewarding. Regularly celebrating these small victories keeps motivation alive, especially in areas where your child may not naturally excel but is putting in the effort to improve.

Creating a culture of praise within the family involves more than occasional compliments; it requires a consistent approach to recognizing and appreciating effort, regardless of the outcome. This can be achieved by taking time to reflect on each family member's contributions and achievements, perhaps during weekly family meetings or casual conversations. Discuss not just what was accomplished, but how it was accomplished, emphasizing the creativity, perseverance, or courage involved. This practice helps shift the focus from outcome-based recognition to effort-based praise, which is crucial in fostering resilience and a growth mindset. When teens realize that their efforts are valued regardless of the result, they are more likely to take on challenges and persist in the face of difficulties.

Using encouragement as motivation is closely tied to how praise is articulated. Positive reinforcement, when used effectively, can boost a teen's willingness to keep pushing through challenges. It's about catching them in the act of figuring things out and reinforcing that behavior with positive feedback that is specific and timely. For example, if you notice your teen is making an effort to keep their room organized, a specific compliment like, "I really appreciate how you've kept your room tidy this week; it makes the whole house feel nicer," can be more motivating than a generic "good job." This specificity not only makes the praise more genuine but also directs your teen to the behaviors that are valued and expected. Additionally, coupling praise with tangible rewards that align with your family values—like extra privileges or choice-based incentives—can motivate teens to maintain their positive behaviors.

Reflecting on growth regularly is another crucial component of celebrating progress. This involves looking back over time to recognize the developments and changes that have occurred. It can be facilitated through family discussions, where each member shares their personal growth highlights and challenges, or through private journals that record thoughts and experiences over time. These reflections allow teens to see for themselves how far they've come, making the abstract concept of growth more concrete and recognizable. They provide a sense of progression that can be incredibly satisfying and motivating. Moreover, these reflections offer valuable insights into the areas where they still need support, allowing you as a parent to better understand how you can aid their ongoing development.

Resources for Further Support: Where to Turn When You Need Help

Navigating adolescence is a complex process filled with unique challenges and milestones. While parents and caregivers provide a primary layer of support, there are times when professional assistance becomes necessary to ensure a teenager's well-being. Understanding when and how to seek this help is crucial.

Identifying when professional help is needed is the first step in ensuring your teen's well-being. Look for signs that might indicate a need for professional intervention. These signs can vary widely, ranging from persistent feelings of sadness or anxiety that disrupt daily activities to noticeable changes in behavior such as withdrawal from social connections, drastic changes in eating or sleeping patterns, or unexplained declines in academic performance.

Finding the right resources is essential when such signs emerge. It's important to take action by seeking out professionals who specialize in adolescent issues. Finding the right therapist or counselor can feel overwhelming, but it starts with a few key steps. You might begin by consulting your family doctor, who can provide a referral, or by using trusted resources like the American Psychological Association's psychologist locator. When choosing a therapist, it's important to consider their specialization in teen treatment and approach to therapy, ensuring it aligns with your teen's needs and your family's values. Additionally, involving your teen in the selection process can empower them and enhance their comfort level with the treatment process.

Utilizing school resources can often serve as valuable support systems and provide immediate assistance. Most schools have trained guidance counselors who understand the intricacies of adolescent life and are equipped to provide short-term counseling, crisis intervention, and referrals to longer-term support if necessary. Additionally, many schools have peer support programs and other initiatives designed to promote mental well-being among students. Familiarizing yourself and your teen with these resources can provide them with additional layers of support that are readily accessible in their daily environment.

Online and community resources offer a wealth of tools that can be valuable in supporting teenagers and parents. Websites like Teen Mental Health or Young Minds offer a plethora of information, including articles, toolkits, and contact information for crisis services. Online forums and support groups can also offer anonymity and accessibility, providing both teens and parents with a platform to share experiences and solutions in a supportive setting. However, it's crucial to vet these online resources carefully to ensure they are reputable and provide accurate, helpful information.

As you incorporate these resources into your support strategy, remember that every teen's needs are unique. What works for one may not work for another, and sometimes finding the right support can take time. The key is persistence and open communication, ensuring your teen feels supported and heard throughout the process. By utilizing a combination of personal support, professional help, and educational resources, you can create a comprehensive support system that empowers your teen to navigate the challenges of adolescence with greater resilience and confidence.

## A Chance to Pay It Forward

As you turn the last pages of this book, please take a moment to hold the door open for someone else – for another parent that may be experiencing similar challenges with their teen.

Simply by sharing one to two sentences about your own journey with your teen, you'll show new readers where they can find all the guidance they need to enhance their teens' social skills too.

**Please scan the QR code to leave a review.**

Thank you so much for your support. We're all on our own parenting journeys, but every ounce of help we can share makes a huge impact to our future generation.

# Conclusion

We've made it! From decoding the impact of smartphones on socializing to navigating the treacherous waters of social anxiety, we've covered it all. We've explored how to build those crucial social skills, the ones that'll help your teen navigate life without constantly feeling like they're starring in their own personal awkward sitcom.

Remember when we talked about communication, empathy, emotional regulation, resilience, conflict resolution, active listening, and self-esteem? Those aren't just fancy words to impress at dinner parties. These are the superpowers your teen needs to conquer their social world. Think of them as the Avengers of social skills, each one powerful on its own, but unstoppable when combined.

Now, let's talk about those exercises throughout the book. They're not just there to fill space or give you an excuse to spend more time with your teen (although that's a nice bonus). These activities are your secret weapon in understanding and bonding with your teen. They're like a cheat code for parenting, but without the guilt of actually cheating.

This book isn't just about giving you a bunch of information to file away in your "I'll get to it someday" folder. It's about empowering you to be the superhero sidekick in your teen's journey. We're equipping you with the knowledge and strategies to support your teen's social development effectively. Think of yourself as the Alfred to their Batman, the Q to their James Bond, the... well, you get the idea.

But here's the thing, the social landscape is always changing. What's cool today might be cringe-worthy tomorrow. (Just ask anyone who still says "groovy".) That's why it's crucial to stay open, adaptable, and proactive. Keep learning, keep adjusting, and for the love of all that is holy, please try to understand what TikTok is.

Now, here's your call to action: Don't just read this book and put it on a shelf to gather dust. Use it! Engage with the activities, try out the strategies, create that supportive environment. Your teen's future self will thank you (even if their current self rolls their eyes at you).

Remember, you've got this! With the right tools and mindset, you can help your teen navigate the complexities of social interactions with the grace of a... well, maybe not a swan, but at least a slightly clumsy duckling. And that's progress!

If you're feeling overwhelmed (and let's face it, who isn't?), don't worry. There are plenty of resources out there to help you on this journey. Check out online forums, community programs, or professional services. It takes a village to raise a child, and in the digital age, that village might just be a Facebook group.

Before we wrap this up, I want to get a little personal. As someone who's passionate about helping parents and teens navigate the social challenges of the digital age, I want to thank you. Thank you for caring enough to read this book, for wanting to understand and support your teen, and for embarking on this important journey. Your dedication to improving your teen's life is truly inspiring.

So, let's keep this conversation going. Let's work together to build a future where our teens can confidently and empathetically engage with the world around them. Because at the end of the day, that's what it's all about - raising kids who aren't just socially savvy, but kind, empathetic, and ready to take on the world.

Here's to you, to your teens, and to a future filled with meaningful connections and fewer awkward silences.

With gratitude and a shared eye roll at dad jokes,

*Amber Preston*

# References

Cavaness, K., Picchioni, A., & Fleshman, J. W. (2020). Linking Emotional Intelligence to Successful Health Care Leadership: The Big Five Model of Personality. *Clinics in Colon and Rectal Surgery, 33*(04), 195–203. NCBI. https://doi.org/10.1055/s-0040-1709435

Dweck, C. (2012). *Mindset: How You Can Fulfill Your Potential.* Robinson.

Leigh, E., & Clark, D. M. (2018). Understanding Social Anxiety Disorder in Adolescents and Improving Treatment Outcomes: Applying the Cognitive Model of Clark and Wells (1995). *Clinical Child and Family Psychology Review, 21*(3), 388–414. https://doi.org/10.1007/s10567-018-0258-5

www.ingramcontent.com/pod-product-compliance
Lightning Source LLC
Chambersburg PA
CBHW021104130626
46554CB00002B/516

* 9 7 9 8 9 9 0 0 9 8 9 4 7 *